MW01028390

CourseBook Series

The CourseBook Series is the product of Dr. Mark H. Kavanaugh. Dr. Kavanaugh is a Professor of Psychology and Social Sciences at Kennebec Valley Community College. The CourseBooks contain the teaching content for each course.

Format

While definitively designed for digital distribution, each CourseBook is available in a number of formats. Distribution of the multi-touch ebook version is done exclusively through Apple Books. These CourseBooks may be purchased and downloaded directly to any iOS or Mac device.

Print versions of the CourseBooks are also available and are distributed through Amazon Kindle Unlimited.

Editing and Errors

Dr. Kavanaugh has written and edited all of this material but he is a horrible editor. He also cannot afford to have the work professionally reviewed. Mistakes, misspellings, broken links, and other errors may exist. Readers are encouraged to contact Dr. Kavanaugh directly to inform him of these errors for the next edition!

Copyright and Use

Index

Chapter 1 - The Psychology of Adulthood

Chapter 2 - Conceptual Models

Chapter 3 - Transitions into Adulthood

Chapter 4 - Emerging Adulthood

Chapter 5 - Young Adulthood

Chapter 6 - Family, Work, and Education

Chapter 7 - Love and Intimacy

Chapter 8 - Generativity

Chapter 9 - Midlife Events

Chapter 10 - Adult Sexuality

Chapter 11 - Plan B

Chapter 12 - Late Adulthood

Chapter 13 - Changing Roles

Chapter 14 - End of Life

Chapter 15 - The Search for Meaning

Special Assignments

Planning to Age Well

How this CourseBook Works

The content of this CourseBook aligns with activities, expectations, and assignments that are found in the KVCC Learning Management System (LMS).

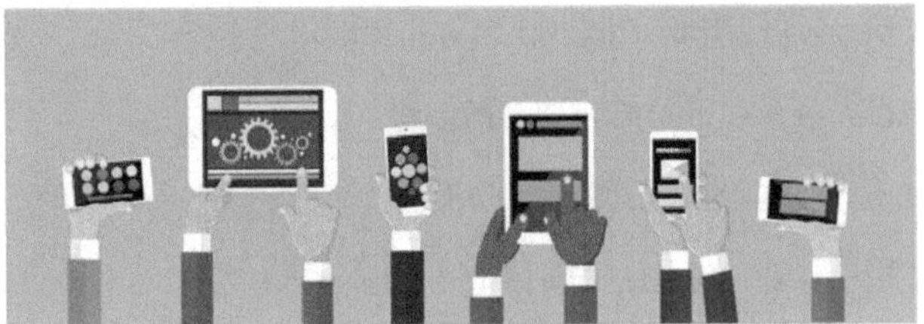

Students are expected to read and absorb the information in the CourseBook, read and review any textbook or other reading assignments, review the Assessment expectations outlined in each CourseBook Chapter, and participate in the expectations set by the instructor of the course in the LMS.

Chapter Organization

Each Chapter has been organized using an instructional design model called ALOTA, provides an outline of course materials that adheres to long-standing instructional design theory for adult learners. ALOTA is a personal creation of mine but it is greatly influenced by Gagne's Nine Events of Instruction

ALOTA

ALOTA is an acronym for the four essential parts of a lesson plan (or, in this case, chapter):

Attention
Learning Outcomes
Teaching
Assessment

Each Chapter in the CourseBooks series is organized in this manner in order to guide students through the material they are expected to learn.

Attention

Images, videos, text, and/or activities that bring readers into the focus of the lesson.

Learning Outcomes

Adhering to the language of Blooms Taxonomy of Learning Objectives, this section outlines the performance-based learning outcomes for the lesson. These align with the Assessment section of each lesson.

Teaching

This section can contain any variety of resources including text, lectures, recordings, videos, and links that provide a pathway through material to assist students in readying themselves for the Assessments.

Assessments

This section outlines assignments for students to demonstrate learning. In my courses there are generally three types of assessments:

- Online Discussions - Interactive message boards that allow students to post a response to an instructor's prompt, view others' responses, and interact with other students.
- Quizzes - These contain different types of questions depending on the level of learning I want them to measure. Types of questions include: multiple choice, short answer, essay, matching, and others.
- Assignments - These usually require that the student submit a document of some kind. Often this is a paper, but it may also be a presentation, video, recorded speech, etc.

QR Codes

In order to ensure that readers of the print version of this CourseBook can still access online content, I have included QR Codes.

Most smart phones are able to scan these codes with their camera and access the online material!

Outcomes Alignment

Alignment with the APA Guidelines

The American Psychological Association (APA) produces guidelines for the development of curriculum in the teaching of Psychology at the undergraduate level.

Here is a link to that document

The CourseBook series is designed to outline instructional materials and activities that demonstrate competence and knowledge in Psychology in alignment with these guidelines.

Below is a list of these outcomes. In red, you will find the unique set of assessments from this course that are specifically designed to address this outcome. Not all of the APA outcomes will be addressed in a single class, but they are addressed throughout the curriculum.

Content Knowledge and Application

- Describe key concepts, principles, and theories in psychological science
- Develop a working knowledge of psychology's major subfields
    - Chapter 2 Assignment - Theories
- Portray significant aspects of the history of psychological science
- Apply psychological content to solve practical problems
    - Chapter 7 Assignment - Relationships
- Provide examples of psychology's integrative themes
    - Chapter 5 Assignment - Affirmation

Scientific Inquiry and Critical Thinking

- Exercise scientific reasoning to investigate psychological phenomena
- Interpret, design, and evaluate psychological research
- Incorporate sociocultural factors in scientific research practices
    - Chapter 3 Assignment - Adult?
- Use statistics to evaluate quantitative research findings

Values in Psychological Science

- Employ ethical standards in research, practice, and academic contexts
- Develop and practice interpersonal and intercultural responsiveness
- Apply psychological principles to strengthen community and improve quality of life

Communication, Psychological Literacy, and Technology Skills

- Interact effectively with others
- Write and present effectively for different purposes
- Provide evidence of psychological literacy
  - Chapter 4 Assignment - Article
- Exhibit appropriate technological skills to improve communication

Personal and Professional Development

- Exhibit effective self-regulation
- Refine project management skills
- Display effective judgment in professional interactions
- Cultivate workforce collaboration skills
- Demonstrate appropriate workforce technological skills
  - Chapter 8 Assignment - Selves
- Develop direction for life after graduation
  - Chapter 6 Assignment - School/Career

Alignment with the AAC&U VALUE Rubrics

In addition to the Learning Outcomes associated with the APA, specific to the field of Psychology, the Department has adopted additional learning outcomes as pretend in the structure of the VALUE Rubrics produced by the Association of American Colleges & Universities (AAC&U).

VALUE stands for "Value Added Learning for Undergraduate Education" and represents a national standard for the learning that should occur in undergraduate programs.

Below is a list of the specific expectations in this course that align with these outcomes.

Civic Engagement

Creative Thinking

- Chapter 14 Assignment - Obituary

Critical Thinking

Ethical Reasoning

Foundational Skills for Lifelong Learning

Global Learning

Information Literacy

- Chapter 4 Assignment - Article

Inquiry and Analysis

Integrative Learning

- Chapter 11 Assignment - Resilience

Intercultural Knowledge

- Chapter 3 Assignment - Norms

Interpersonal Communication

Oral Communication

- Chapter 8 Assignment - Selves

Problem Solving

- Special Assignment - Planning to Age Well

Quantitative Literacy

Reading

Teamwork

Written Communication

- Chapter 15 Assignment - Obituary

Adult Development

The course offers students the opportunity to study biopsychosocial changes across adulthood from applied and theoretical perspectives. Building on previous studies in Developmental Sciences, students examine findings and theories related to identity, social affiliations, styles of coping and states of mind throughout adulthood. The last sections of the course allows students to develop informed points of view on the meaning of aging.

Changes made to this Edition of the CourseBook

1. Alignment with new APA Learning Outcomes.
2. Added QR Codes to all links.
3. Converted in-text videos to full page.
4. Chapter 1 - Removed question regarding what students are looking forward to from the quiz.

5. Chapter 2 - Changed discussion to focus on meaning to be found in theories.
6. Chapter 2 - Added assignment that focuses on reflection on each of the primary theories in this Chapter.
7. Chapter 5 - Changed quiz into an assignment on the affirmation of adult identity.
8. Chapter 7 - Expanded on explanation of the changes related to intimacy in young adulthood.
9. Chapter 8 - Replaced discussion with an assignment on Roger's Psychology of the Self.
10. Chapter 10 - Deleted discussion.
11. Chapter 12 - Modified discussion and deleted the Chapter 12 Quiz
12. General Edits and Clean Up

About the Author

Mark H. Kavanaugh, Ph.D.

Mark Kavanaugh has been writing, teaching, and integrating technology into instruction for decades. He holds a Masters in Counseling, Masters in Instructional and Performance Technology, and a Ph.D. in Educational Psychology. Mark lives in Maine with his wife Katie.

Visit Mark's Website

1 The Psychology of Adulthood

Attention

What is Normal?

This book, as you will see, focuses on **normative development**, the patterns and trends that are common to the most people. But, what really is normal? We know that within the concept of **normal** is a LOT of diversity. Two people can be very different and both can still be considered "normal." Here is how the field of Psychology approaches the concept of normal.

Since "normal" is common, we can understand what is normal by understanding what is "abnormal."

We define abnormal based on three criteria:

1. **Statistics** - abnormal behavior is rare. Less than 2% of the population.
2. **Social Norms** - abnormal behavior violates the expectations of someone's culture.

3. **Dysfunction** - abnormal behavior interferes with the individuals functioning in their role in society.

Pretty much all three of these may need to be met for a behavior to be considered “abnormal” This does not mean that behaviors that don’t meet these criteria are not, at times problematic, but they would not meet this strict criteria.

Learning Outcomes

Upon completion of this Chapter, students should be able to:

1. Discuss examples of the Developmental Clocks (Biological, Psychological, Social, and Historical)
2. Apply the Developmental Perspective to a psychological question.

Teaching

Note on Teaching: This section will describe all the material that you ned to review to complete the Assessment section successfully. While this section is akin to a "Lecture" in class, not all the information you need to complete the assessments are contained in these pages. Other sources such as your textbook, Online resources, movies, etc. may need to be reviewed.

The Developmental Perspective

Through this course you are going to be learning how to take the "Developmental Perspective" or DP.

The DP is very simple. When we are faced with a question in Psychology we affirm that the answer to that question may very well be impacted by how OLD the person is.

In this class we will be studying what NORMALLY happens across the lifespan and based on that knowledge we can take the DP on any topic. Here are some examples:

"How does divorce affect the children?"

This is obviously a great question, but for this class it is incomplete. Before we can really answer this question we need to know how old the kids are. We know that changes in family structure can have profound impacts on an individual but these impacts will be different based on how old the person is.

Let's say the person we are asking this about is 10 years old. What is "normally" going on in the life of a 10-year old that may be impacted by a divorce?

What if the person we are asking this about is 17? What if they are 25? What if they are 50? (Remember, a divorce can happen at any time in the lifespan). It should be apparent to you now that it is quite difficult to answer a question without asking how old the person is.

Note: Taking the DP is not the same as applying Developmental Theory. You are NOT taking the DP when you ask something like "How does intelligence change over childhood?" or if you ask "How does memory change in late adulthood?" These are simply applications of theory and knowledge.

The DP **adds age** to the equation of a question that is not about age. So we ask questions like these:

1. How well do people remember things?
2. How fast can a person learn a new skill?
3. How will losing a job impact a person?
4. How will having children impact a person's plans?
5. How will a serious injury impact someone?

The answer to each of these questions is the same - It depends on how old the person is!

So, to apply the DP to each of these questions, we would rewrite them as follows (and these are just examples, you can apply any age...)

1. How well does a 3 year old remember things?
2. How fast can a 12 year old learn a new skill?
3. How will losing a job impact a 55 year old?

4. How will having children impact a 13 year old's plans?
5. How will a serious injury impact 6 year old?

Normative Development

This course is going to focus on normative development. We are going to explore the ways in which people normally change over time. That way when you know how old a person is, you can simply look at your Developmental Psychology class and see where they should be in terms of memory, emotions, social interactions, etc. That way you can use this information to guide your practice.

We are going to be looking at the following areas of normative development:

1. Normative age-graded influences - changes that occur because of maturation, genetic influences, that are common among all people of a certain age.
2. Normative history-graded influences - changes due to the **cohort** you were born into. This is based on the year you were born. (We will go a bit more into this when we talk about the **Historical Clock**)
3. Non-normative life influences - these are the occurrences of things in our lives at specific ages and how it may impact our development.

Developmental
Perspective

MOVIE - Developmental Perspective

Developmental Clocks

Your book refers to these as ages, whereas I am going to refer to them as the **Developmental Clocks**. When we consider that we are continually aging we can imagine a clock ticking away as time goes by in our lives.

The truth is, we have multiple clocks ticking at the same time. Each of these are marking time in different areas of our development and in different influences on our development.

Biological Clock

You are probably already familiar with this one! The biological clock represents the maturation of our bodies and minds through the genetic time table. The biological clock determines when we will learn to go potty, when we can have children, our first gray hair, and when we will die.

We might hear about the Biological Clock when we consider women who are thinking of having children. There is a time frame during which this is possible (and more safe.)

Psychological Clock

The Psychological Clock is the one that marks time in the development of our emotions, emotional control, cognitive abilities (thinking, memory, learning, etc.) and our maturity.

Already you might be noting that sometimes the Biological Clock and the Psychological Clock are not always in sync! We all know someone who is unusually mature and responsible "for their age" and we all know someone who is not as "mature" as they should be for their age!

Social Clock

The "should" mentioned above could also be seen as part of the Social Clock. The Social Clock marks out what you SHOULD be able to do or be doing at a particular age based on the social norms and values of a culture.

It may be that in your family it was expected that you would move out of the home, get a job (or go to school), and start your life right around the age of 18-21. If you were 35 years old and still living at home, still dependent on your parents, this would be seen as "wrong" and in violation of the expectations of your culture. This would be a violation of the Social Clock.

Historical Clock

A very popular way of characterizing the different Historical Clocks is by the use of the concept of Generations. Here is a great website that outlines the Generations from the point of view of marketing.

Generations X, Y, Z, and the Others

We are all born into what Sociologists call a "Generation."

1. Silent Generation - born between 1928 and 1945.
2. Baby Boomers - born between 1946 and 1964.

3. Generation X - born between 1965 and 1980.
4. Millennials (Generation Y) - born between 1980 and 1995.
5. Generation Z - born between 1995 and 2010.
6. Generation Alpha - born after 2011.

Based on research, we know that these generations share certain characteristics. However, it is important to remember that these characteristics are statistical similarities...there is a lot of variability within each of these groups. So, they are not meant to be "prescriptive" - meaning, because you are a Millennial, you need to be like this...

Adult Development

Of course this class is focused on development after we have become adults (or at least after we THINK we have become adults!

In this class we will examine some theories that cover the whole lifespan and we might go back into childhood a bit to see the context by which these later stags come about. At other times we will be looking at models and research specific to events and experiences that are only found in adulthood.

Throughout I will refer to the basic concepts of the Developmental Perspective and the various clocks. These will be the unifying themes throughout the course.

This content will be explored in the following Chapters:

Chapter 2 - Conceptual Models

This chapter will explore the various lifespan theories and major thoughts on Adult Development. We will be revisiting some of these throughout the content.

Chapter 3 - Transitions into Adulthood

What does it mean to be an adult? How have we celebrated the entrance into adulthood across history and

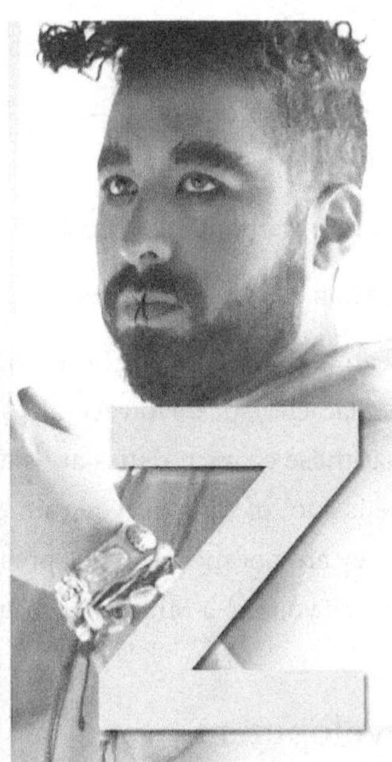

MOVIE - Generations Throughout History

around the world? We will explore how we define adulthood and how we find out when we made it.

Chapter 4 - Emerging Adulthood

Erikson and others have mostly aligned the entrance into adulthood as the stage that follows adolescence. Not so fast. We will be exploring a NEW stage that has evolved in-between adolescence and full adulthood where we have an extended period of "not quite fully adultness."

Chapter 5 - Young Adulthood

Successfully transitioning into adulthood...now what do we do? Family, work, and other priorities begin to be a part of our lives. Or, maybe we hike the Appalachian Trail.

Chapter 6 - Family, Work, and Education

These three areas, at least in the US, define a lot of who we see ourselves as. These are social status symbols as well. How do we make a family work? How about career development? Do we go to school? We will explore these decisions and transitions.

Chapter 7 - Love and Intimacy

This one is important enough to have its own chapter! We will explore models of relationships with friends, family, and, in many cases, romantic partners. Do we choose our friends wisely? What impacts these choices? I have a couple theories of my own about that!

Chapter 8 - Generativity

According to Erikson, this is where we make our imprint on the world, where we make our legacy. How do we go about living up to our own expectations? How do we set and attain goals? Why is the so important to us?

Chapter 9 - Midlife Events

It might not be a "crisis", but it is certainly an event! Or maybe, more than one event. At times we come face to face with our own mortality. How can this be a thrilling change of course or a dangerous fall into egotism? We'll find out!

Chapter 10 - Adult Sexuality

In this Chapter we will explore sexuality as it manifests throughout adulthood. We ask why the peak in sexuality occurs at different ages in men and women, we explore how sexuality changes with age (in some ways) and then I'll show you why sex is similar to riding a bicycle (and it has little to do with remembering how to do it!)

Chapter 11 - Plan B

When we look forward in our lives we often have expectations of how things will work out, our plans. What if things go off the tracks? In this Chapter we will explore the impact of illness, disease, divorce, death, and other factors that force us to abandon our plans and make new ones.

Chapter 12 - Late Adulthood

Just like we explored what it means to be an adult, we have to ask what it means to be old. Why do we age at all? What forces are at work here (including gravity and time!) Can our decline also be an ascension?

Chapter 13 - Changing Roles

Important changes are afoot in late life. Changes in our social statuses and our role in the world. What does this look like around the world? Where is our place in our world? Do we still have much to offer? Will the world let us offer it?

Chapter 14 - End of Life

You know the saying, the only thing you can really depend on are death and taxes. Well, this is not a business class, so we will talk about death. It is a universal shared experience and yet it can challenge us like nothing else. What is a "good death"? How have all the decisions we have made so far led us to these final days? How do we plan our death?

Chapter 15 - The Search for Meaning

We end our exploration with a nearly universal question, what is all this for? What is it about? Is there something after this? Do we get to do this again or is this a one-way trip? How can we live every moment like it might be the last without becoming narcissists? What art are you going to leave behind that will document a life well lived?

Are you ready?

Let's go...

Assessment

This section describes the activities and assignments associated with this Chapter. Be sure to check with your instructor as to which ones you are expected to complete.

Note regarding Discussions: These activities are primarily geared toward students who are taking the course in either an Online or Hybrid format. It is expected that students will post an answer to the prompt contained in the section below and reply to at least two other students' posts in order to obtain full credit for the discussion. All posts must be substantive and contribute to the discussion.

Note regarding Assignments: These activities entail the creation of a "document" of sorts that needs to be sent to your instructor. Most of these may be papers. All papers must be submitted to the identified "Drop Box" for the assignment and must be in either Microsoft Word or PDF format. Pay attention to expectations such as title pages and APA formatting if these are indicated in the instructions.

Other assignments may entail different types of "documents" including presentations, artwork, charts, spreadsheets, and/or movies. Instructions on how to submit these will be included in the descriptions below

Though they will not be repeated, all of the above notes should be assumed in subsequent chapters, unless otherwise indicated.

Chapter 1 Discussion

In this discussion I want you to provide an example of ONE clock and how it manifests in your life. You can tell a story or simply state a fact about yourself. Here are some examples:

1. I was born during the "Cold War" when the threat of Nuclear War was very present and on our minds. This is part of my Historical Clock and impacts the way I view the world.
2. I had my first child when I was in my early 30's. This makes me an older father than some other fathers. This could be an example of Biological or Social clock...according to the social clock I "should" have had kids by then!

Just post ONE example of ONE clock. Respond to each other's postings as appropriate.

Chapter 1 Quiz

1. Write a typical psychological question. Then, write that same question again but apply an example of the Developmental Perspective.

Conceptual Models

Attention

Theories, Models, and Research ...OH MY!

Over time the field of psychology has produced some important theories that will be valuable through our journey in this class. Many of these ideas have been around for quite some time. The reason they are still around is probably because they are well-founded and accurate portrayals of our lived experience.

Research in psychology usually starts out with a phenomenon that has caught the eye of a researcher, and the researcher asks the same question that you do...

Why did they do that?

Charged with the need to understand human behavior, the researcher begins to do what they do best...look for answers. They do this by engaging in a very systematic and disciplined method.

Step 1 - What exactly are we looking at.

We make observations to help us define what factors are involved in the mystery we are trying to solve.

Step 2 - What do we already know?

This is called the Literature Review. What do we already have data on? What terms are used in the psychological literature to describe what we are seeing.

We may, in fact, find our solution here!

Step 3 - Find the gap.

If we don't find our answer, we identify the gap in knowledge and plan to fill that gap with new knowledge.

Step 4 - Identify Factors (Variables)

Clearly identify and measure the factors that are involved in the situation.

Step 5 - Collect Data on Relationships

We then collect data, conduct experiments, look at existing records, make detailed observation, etc. and examine this data for any relationships (correlation or cause-effect) between the variables.

Step 6 - Theory or Model Building

Write out the conclusions of our work in the form of a model or theory that provides an explanation of the behaviors and the different factors that are involved.

The theories and models that explain human development in this chapter (and in subsequent chapters) have been developed largely through this process.

Learning Outcomes

Upon completion of this Chapter, students should be able to:

1. Review theories for evidence of personal meaning.
2. Apply various theories of human development.

Teaching

Where to start?

As I approach this Chapter, I have wondered how I'm going to be able to communicate a set of important ideas that will guide our exploration of adult development from here on. Let me try and put these in context.

Human defy explanation!

What I mean by this is that the study of human behavior is different than most other scientific endeavors. In most of the other sciences we are seeking the laws of nature that produce what we observe. With the occasional distraction of theoretical physics and quantum mechanics, once we find the laws, our observations continue to be consistent with the laws. This validates our description of the laws and provides us with a relatively predictable world view.

Psychology…not so much!

When we study human behavior we run into a wall trying to find "laws" in the same way we find laws in other areas of science. This is a reflection of how different we are from other citizens of the natural world.

When I first began my formal education in science (Marine Biology) I had a distinct distaste for the social sciences because of this. Although I never really dismissed its scientific nature, I certainly questioned its utility when it was unable to produce reliable predictions! Chemistry, Math, Physics, and Biology were the real sciences.

I won't go into my own evolution into a fanboy for all things psychology, but eventually, it was the difficulty of nailing down and predicting human behavior that lured me into its cognitive clutches. (That and Dr. John Bridge, the Faculty Advisor for the Ultimate Frisbee team I was on...we all have our paths!)

In psychology, we don't have many laws of behavior, but we do have a lot of theories. These are models that endeavor to meet the goals of the field; to describe, explain, predict, and ultimately control human behavior.

Since human behavior escapes out of all the boxes we have tried to put it in, we have to have a lot of different boxes. In support of this notion, I'm going to say that there is no perfect box, but that all of these boxes are good boxes and have their season. We learn them all because at different times our particular observations need to be put into a particular box. It won't stay there, but we can observe it for a while it is there. Much like the presence of famous wizards on the cards found in Harry Potter's Chocolate Frog packages.

So, I present to you some of my favorite theories that we will have the opportunity to apply to different aspects of adult development through this course. This is MY list and other writers may choose to use others and may dismiss my use of some of these. Too bad, this is my book.

I have found these models to be useful in understanding my own behavior and the behavior of others around me and they have served me well. They are not perfect for all occasions, but Batman didn't only have one tool in his utility belt!

Let's get started on building your Psychological Human Development Utility Belt!

Psychosocial Development

For me, the work of Erik Erikson stands out from the rest. I have a deep interest in identity development and his departure from his mentor, Sigmund Freud, to embrace psychological development across the lifespan signaled a major leap forward in the field.

Erikson actually coined the term Psychosocial as a departure from Freud's "Psychosexual" stages. Erikson believed that humans develop in a social context and encounter a predictable sequence of dilemmas that they need to resolve. They are dilemmas to the point that the emerging psychology (psycho-) has to come to terms with the norms, values, and expectations of the sociocultural environment in which it is developing (social)...hence the term psychosocial development.

Erikson was apparently a great personality. Erik was also a tall, blonde, blue eyed Jew. He was teased at the temple for being Nordic and teased at grammar school for being Jewish. No wonder her came up with a theory of identity development!

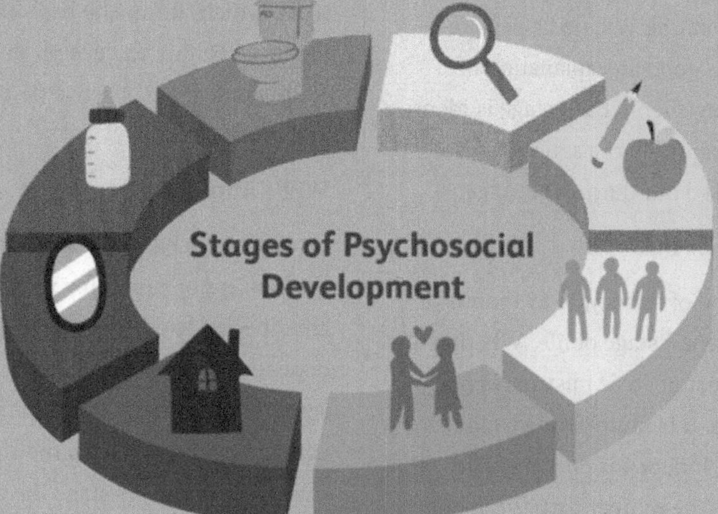

Early Childhood
autonomy vs. shame and doubt
Preschool
initiative vs. guilt
Infancy
trust
vs.
mistrust
School Age
industry
vs.
inferiority
Stages of Psychosocial
Development
Maturity
ego integrity
vs.
despair
Adolescence
identity
vs.
role confusion
Middle Adulthood
generativity vs. stagnation
Young Adulthood
intimacy vs. isolation

Erikson's theory posits that we go through 8 critical dilemmas in our life where we interact with our environment and build our identity and our place in society.

The following is quoted from the Wikipedia page regarding his theory and it as good an explanation of these stages as I've seen anywhere. Each stage is identified by the Virtue that is gained by the stage and the dilemma itself that is worked out during the stage.

Hope - Basic trust vs. basic mistrust

This stage covers the period of infancy, 0–18 months, which is the most fundamental stage of life. Whether the baby develops basic trust or basic mistrust is not merely a matter of nurture. It is multi-faceted and has strong social components. It depends on the quality of the maternal relationship. The mother carries out and reflects her inner perceptions of trustworthiness, a sense of personal meaning, etc. on the child. An important part of this stage is providing stable and constant care of the infant. This helps the child develop trust that can transition into relationships other than parental. Additionally, children develop trust in others to support them. If successful in this, the baby develops a sense of trust, which "forms the basis in the child for a sense of identity." Failure to develop this trust will result in a feeling of fear and a sense that the world is inconsistent and unpredictable.

Will - Autonomy vs. shame

Covers early childhood around 1–3 years old. Introduces the concept of autonomy vs. shame and doubt. The child begins to discover the beginnings of his or her independence, and parents must facilitate the child's sense of doing basic tasks "all by himself/herself." Discouragement can lead to the child doubting his or her efficacy. During this stage the child is usually trying to master toilet training. Additionally, the child discovers his talents or abilities, and it is important to ensure the child is able to explore those activities. Erikson states it is essential to allow the children freedom in exploration but also create an environment welcoming of failures. Therefore, the parent should not punish or reprimand the child for failing at the task. Shame and doubt occurs when the child feels incompetent in ability to complete tasks and survive. Will is achieved with success of the stage. Children successful in this stage will have "self-control without a loss of self-esteem."

Purpose - Initiative vs. guilt

Preschool / 3–5 years. Does the child have the ability to do things on her own, such as dress herself? Children in this stage are interacting with peers, and creating their own games and activities. If allowed to make these decisions, the child will develop confidence in her ability to lead others. If the child is not allowed to make certain decisions the sense of guilt develops. Guilt in this stage is characterized by a sense of being a burden to others, and the child will therefore usually present herself as a follower. Additionally, the child is asking many questions to build knowledge of the world. If the questions earn responses that are critical and condescending, the child will also develop feelings of guilt. Success in this stage leads to the virtue of purpose, which is the normal balance between the two extremes.

Competence - Industry vs. inferiority

School-age / 6–11 years. Child comparing self-worth to others (such as in a classroom environment). Child can recognize major disparities in personal abilities relative to other children. Erikson places some emphasis on the teacher, who should ensure that children do not feel inferior. During this stage the child's friend group increases in importance in his life. Often during this stage the child will try to prove competency with things rewarded in society, and also develop satisfaction with his abilities. Encouraging the child increases feelings of adequacy and competency in ability to reach goals. Restriction from teachers or parents leads to doubt, questioning, and reluctance in abilities and therefore may not reach full capabilities. Competence, the virtue of this stage, is developed when a healthy balance between the two extremes is reached.

Fidelity - Identity vs. role confusion

Adolescent / 12–18 years. Questioning of self. Who am I? How do I fit in? Where am I going in life? The adolescent is exploring and seeking for her own unique identity. This is done by looking at personal beliefs, goals, and values. The morality of the individual is also explored and developed. Erikson believes that if the parents allow the child to explore, she will determine her own identity. If, however, the parents continually push her to conform to their views, the teen will face identity confusion. The teen is also looking towards the future in terms of employment, relationships, and families. Learning the roles she provides in society is essential since the teen begins to develop the desire to fit in to society. Fidelity is characterized by the ability to commit to others and acceptance of others even with differences. Identity crisis is the result of role confusion and can cause the adolescent to try out different lifestyles.

Love - Intimacy vs. isolation

This is the first stage of adult development. This development usually happens during young adulthood, which is between the ages of 18 to 40. Dating, marriage, family and friendships are important during the stage in their life. This is due to the increase in the growth of intimate relationships with others. By successfully forming loving relationships with other people, individuals are able to experience love and intimacy. They also feel safety, care, and commitment in these relationships. Furthermore, if individuals are able to successfully resolve the crisis of intimacy versus isolation, they are able to achieve the virtue of love. Those who fail to form lasting relationships may feel isolated and alone.

Care - Generativity vs. stagnation

The second stage of adulthood happens between the ages of 40–65. During this time people are normally settled in their lives and know what is important to them. A person is either making progress in his career or treading lightly in his career and unsure if this is what he wants to do for the rest of his working life. Also during this time, if a person is enjoying raising his children and participating in activities, that gives him a sense of purpose. This is one way of contributing to society along with productivity at work and involvement in community activities and organizations. If a person is not comfortable with the way his life is progressing, he's usually regretful about the decisions that he has made in the past and feels a sense of uselessness.

Wisdom - Ego integrity vs. despair

This stage affects the age group of 65 and on. During this time an individual has reached the last chapter in her life and retirement is approaching or has already taken place. Ego-integrity means the acceptance of life in its fullness: the victories and the defeats, what was accomplished and what was not accomplished. Wisdom is the result of successfully accomplishing this final developmental task. Wisdom is defined as "informed and detached concern for life itself in the face of death itself."[39] Having a guilty conscience about the past or failing to accomplish important goals will eventually lead to depression and hopelessness. Achieving the virtue of the stage involves the feeling of living a successful life.

Identity Development

Our next psychologist hails from the great northern country of Canada (like me!). James Marcia is a Canadian psychologist who also took a liking to Erikson's ideas of identity development.

James Marcia

Marcia's theory takes a close look at the ways in which we participate in the development of our identities. Marcia's theory does not move along in stages like Erikson's but describes the lived process of constructing your sense of self over time.

The neat thing about this theory, I think, is that it is continually relevant as we define, and often redefine, our self through the lifespan.

According to his theory, we engage in constructing our identity through two processes that he names "crisis" and "commitment". "Crisis" does NOT refer to the need for a prescription of Ativan, it relates to the process of "looking at the options"...a person looking for a career would be in a "Career Crisis" just as a person looking for a car would be in a "Car Crisis".

"Commitment" refers to the selection of an option. Maybe this is seen best in a relationship example. Dating, you are in crisis, until you find the right one, then you adventure into commitment.

Now consider that you have a lot of parts of your identity and each part has been constructed through different experiences and decisions that you have made that align with crisis and commitment. Marcia's theory states that each piece of our identity can be categorized into one of four areas based on the degree of crisis and commitment involved in that part of our identity.

This table exemplifies the application of Marcia's theory to career development.

IDENTITY FORECLOSURE	IDENTITY MORATORIUM
HIGH commitment towards the prospect of a new career identity but **LOW** exploration activity. Have accepted the prospect of changing careers but unmotivated to start the process of job seeking.	**LOW** commitment to the prospect of a new career identity but **HIGH** level of engagement in exploring new opportunities so are more knowledgeable about possible options.
IDENTITY DIFFUSION	**IDENTITY ACHIEVEMENT**
LOW commitment towards considering a new career. **LOW** motivation to explore new options. Overwhelmed or unaware of number of possibilities so inertia sets in.	**HIGH** commitment to a new career identity and **HIGH** exploration of possible new career options. Accepting of a new career and taking positive action to explore the job market.

Identity Achievement

Areas in our lives where we have looked at the options (crisis) and made a choice (commitment).

Identity Diffusion

Areas in our identity where we are not looking at the options (crisis) and not making choices (commitment). Stuff that is on our "back burner".

Identity Moratorium

Areas in our identity that we are actively working on (crisis) but have not finished or made a choice (commitment).

Identity Foreclosure

Areas in our identity where choices have been made (commitment) but without the benefit of our ability to choose (crisis). Consider this to be the part of your identity that includes your sex, family, and where you lived as a child. It also includes disabilities, trauma events, and family career expectations. A very interesting status to study!

Cognitive Development

You have already experienced my use of the word "construction" in this book. With the advent of the work of our next great scientist, psychology took a great step forward by validating the notion that we play a very important role in the creation of our identity. We actively "construct" our identity (and our internal representations of our world.)

Jean Piaget was not originally a psychologist. Piaget was an ichthyologist, which is a person who studies marine creatures. He has a specialty in mollusks and wrote his first scientific paper at the tender age of 15 (he was a very clever boy!). His work helping Alfred Binet construct an intelligence test led him into a lifelong curiosity in the development of children's minds. His theory, technically referred to as Genetic Epistemology, is his enduring legacy. Genetic Epistemology literally means "the genesis of our ways of knowing the world."

Jean Piaget

Piaget's theory is one that identifies **qualitative** changes in the cognitive capacities of the emerging mind. This is a different approach to other models of cognitive development that measure **quantitative** changes such as memory, attention span, and spatial relations. We will have to get some terms straight.

Schema - a schema is an internal representation of the world. Each of us, for an example, has an internal representation of the concept of "apple". That schema may be relatively simple or extremely complex depending our individual interest and experience with apples.

Assimilation - while many do not believe that humans operate with "instincts" in the strict sense of the word, I believe that assimilation, and accommodation below, are instinctual. Assimilation is the process by which our minds capture facts and observations from our world and store them as schemas. We might create brand new schemas or add to the complexity of existing schemas.

Accommodation - this equally instinctual process, is the method used to modify existing schemas in order to take into consideration (accommodate) new information.

Consider my "apple" example. Here is a nice one...

(and you thought I was going to use an iPhone!)

Early in life you develop a rather simple schema about apple based on your experience and cognitive abilities. Pretty much this is limited to the tasty fruit and the false premise that it somehow keeps doctors away.

As you age and enlarge your world, however, you encounter additional information about apples such as the different types, the fact that apples don't seem to develop on their native trees, that cities can be referred to as the Big Apple (as well as convenience stores) and that somehow one of these things inspired our current knowledge of gravity.

As you age you **assimilate** and **accommodate** your schemas. People with very complex schemas about something are what we call **Experts**.

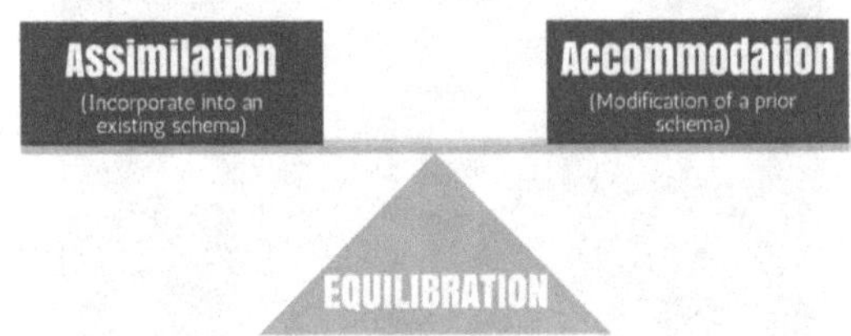

Piaget went further to describe a developmental process of stages that identify the qualitative changes in our ways of knowing across the lifespan.

For our purposes in this class, it is sufficient to understand two things:

1. Adult cognitive demands rarely call upon our Formal Operational abilities, but we can usually do both.

PIAGET'S STAGES OF COGNITIVE DEVELOPMENT

4 FORMAL OPERATIONAL (12 years-adult)

The adolescent can reason abstractly and think in hypothetical terms.

3 CONCRETE OPERATIONAL (7-12 years)

The child can think logically about concrete objects and can thus add and subtract. The child also understands conservation.

2 PREOPERATIONAL (2-6 years)

The child uses symbols (words and images) to represent objects but does not reason logically. The child also has the ability to pretend. During this stage, the child is egocentric.

1 SENSORIMOTOR (0-2 years)

The infant explores the world through direct sensory and motor contact. Object permanence and separation anxiety develop during this stage.

2. When we learn something new, we often go through stages similar to these as our internal schemas become more and more complex.

Intelligence

Close on the tails of Cognitive Development is the notion of Intelligence. Intelligence occupies a special place in the heart of psychology because of its importance and its subsequent resistance to be defined!

There are two major views we might consider when we are thinking about intelligence. One is applicability and the other is talent. Application models of intelligence have to do with context and the skill set needed to be successful in a particular environment.

For instance, IQ, a quotient representing the ratio of our mental age to our chronological age is a fairly good predictor of how well we might do in a typical school situation, but a poor predictor of how well we will get along with others.

Talent approaches to intelligence focus on being really good at something in and of itself. Of course, being really good at school things will help you in school but it will also help in other areas as well.

Triarchic Theory of Intelligence

Our first character in this section is Robert Sternberg. Sternberg's model of intelligence captures these two areas fairly well. He describes three types of intelligence.

Componential Intelligence - This form of intelligence focuses on academic proficiency (similar to an IQ).

Experiential Intelligence - This form of intelligence focuses on the capacity to be intellectually flexible and innovative. In this sense, this is both due to experience but an attitude of flexibility and creativity.

Robert Sternberg

Practical Intelligence - This form of intelligence focuses on the persons ability to adapt, shape, and select behaviors in order to accommodate the demands of a situation. It also encompasses specialized contextual knowledge such as "how to survive in the woods" and "how to build a working combustion engine from popsicle sticks". Stuff not everyone knows!

Howard Gardner

Multiple Intelligences

Another primary, and useful, theory is Howard Gardner's theory of Multiple Intelligence. This set of differ-

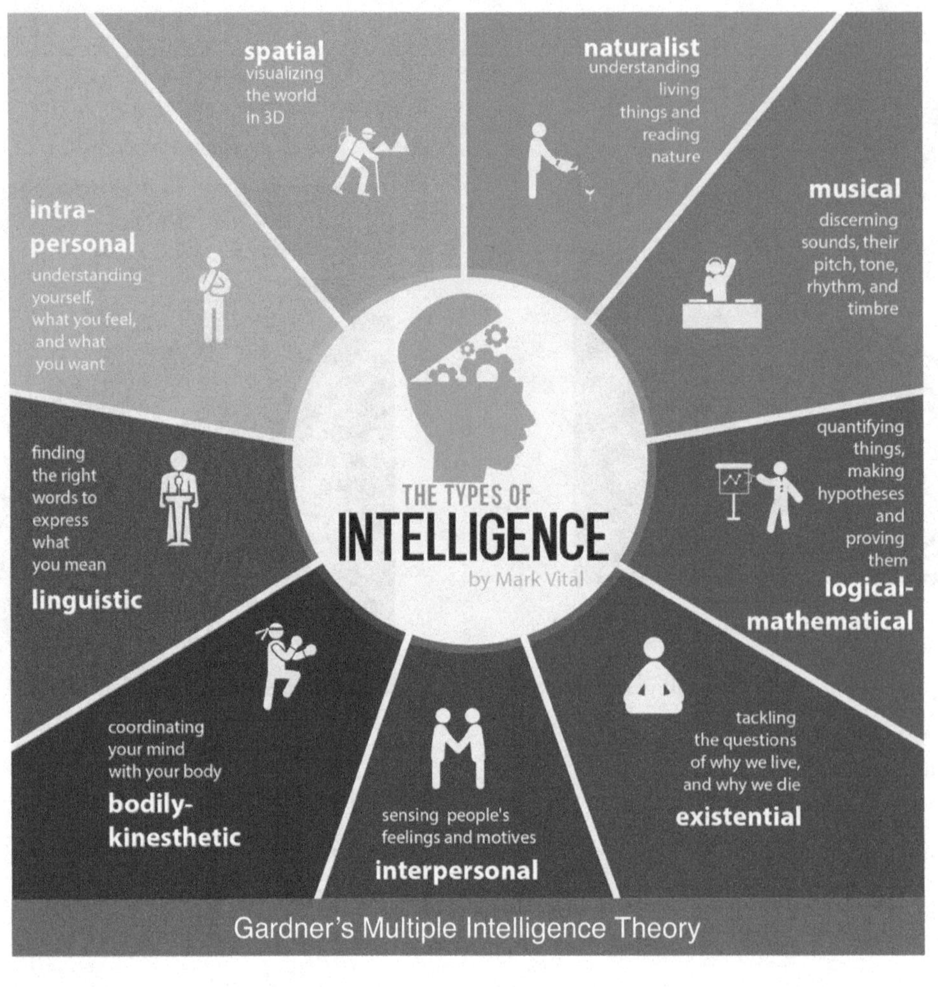
spatial
visualizing the world in 3D
naturalist
understanding living things and reading nature
musical
discerning sounds, their pitch, tone, rhythm, and timbre
intra-personal
understanding yourself, what you feel, and what you want
finding the right words to express what you mean
linguistic
quantifying things, making hypotheses and proving them
logical-mathematical
THE TYPES OF
INTELLIGENCE
by Mark Vital
coordinating your mind with your body
bodily-kinesthetic
sensing people's feelings and motives
interpersonal
tackling the questions of why we live, and why we die
existential
Gardner's Multiple Intelligence Theory

ent kinds of intelligences are largely skill and talent oriented, but provide the widest interpretation of what can be considered "smarts".

Ecological Development

Keeping with the notion of "context" I now want to introduce you to one of the most important, yet widely misunderstood developmental theories.

The term "ecology" refers to the sum total of the interactions of all aspects of a given natural environment. We study natural ecologies in order to understand the "web" of interacting elements associated with that environment and we often observe them as being in a natural balance not worthy of disruption.

Human Ecology looks at naturally occurring social "ecosystems" and analyzes them in similar ways.

Human ecology posits that humans live in interacting social structures of increasing distance from the individual and increasing complexity. Within this concentric model of existence we see ourselves defining and being defined by our experiences as we move out from our family of origin into the social world.

While the theory is descriptive of the human ecosystem in general, it is as important to recognize that the interactions between the components of the system are as important as the individual traveling among them.

This theory comes to us from Urie Brofenbrenner. Interestingly, Urie was a primary contributor to the establishment of Head Start under Sargent Shriver in the 1960s.

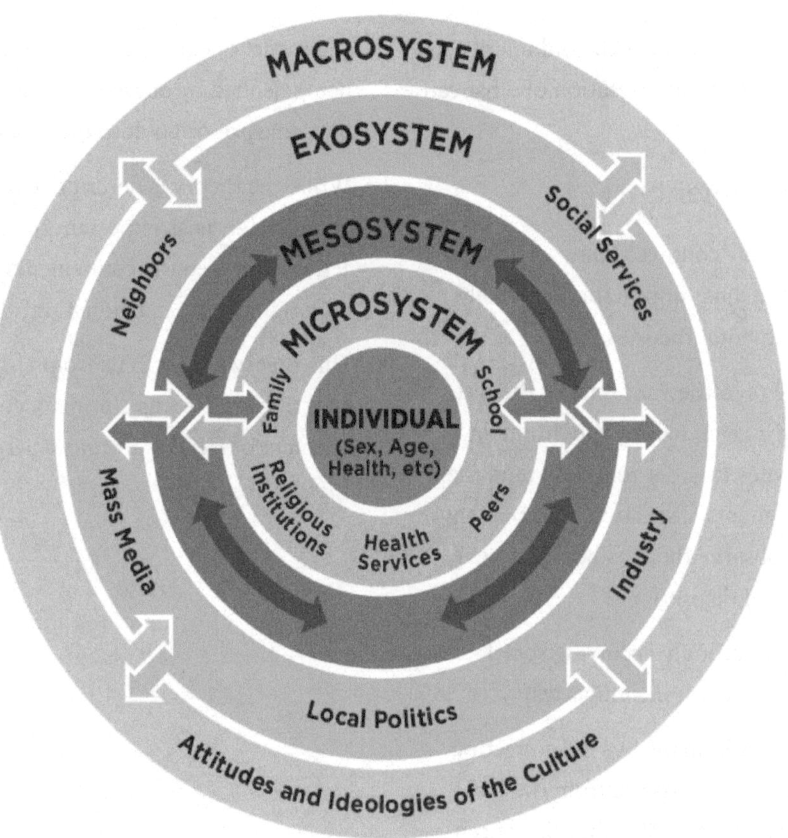
MACROSYSTEM
EXOSYSTEM
MESOSYSTEM
MICROSYSTEM
INDIVIDUAL
(Sex, Age, Health, etc)
Family
School
Religious Institutions
Health Services
Peers
Neighbors
Social Services
Mass Media
Industry
Local Politics
Attitudes and Ideologies of the Culture

Urie Brofenbrenner

Pay close attention to the arrows in this diagram that identify the interactions. In fact, the Mesosystem is considered to be a band that characterizes the entirety of the interactions between larger social structures (Exosystem) and intimate social structures more close to home and more central to our developing identity (Microsystem).

Looking Glass Self

Finally, I want to introduce you to one of my favorite theories and it is not even a theory from psychology! Well, it is more like Social Psychology.

Charles Cooley

Social Psychology is the area of the field that looks at the interaction between our social world and our psychology. Observations of how we behave in groups, how trends in fashion and music change our attitudes, and political rhetoric are just a few areas that are included in this field. Looking Glass Self is a model proposed by famed sociologist, Charles Cooley, regarding the social development of our sense of self.

The basic premise of Cooley's Looking Glass self is fairly simple. Imagine that you are looking into a mirror (looking glass). You see yourself, but not only how you look, but your behavior and all aspects of your character. In the process of determining your personal value and worth, you impinge how important people in your life would consider your observations. How would your mother, father, pastor, best friend, girl/boyfriend, strangers, Jesus, God, your boss, coworkers, etc. interpret the reality of who you are?

Cooly presents that we consider these external views of ourselves and incorporate them into our own perspectives of ourselves. In pragmatic terms, we can easily see how this happens based upon our own experiences. Many of us have probably had individuals in our lives that lifted us up and provided us with a strong and positive sense of self while at the same time, others may have put us down and we can't seem to shake their influence over us, even if they are no longer in our lives!

The Committee

In may own applications of this theory, as you will see in this class, I refer to this "group" of individuals who have the potential to influence our sense of self as the "committee".

It is important to recognize that early in life, some members of our committee are placed on that committee without our say. (Consider this to be Foreclosed aspects of our committee membership from Marcia's theory earlier.)

The Looking Glass Self

How my mom and dad see me.

How my girlfriend sees me.

How my older brother sees me.

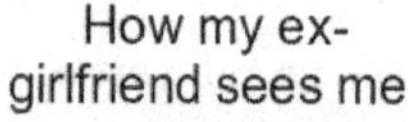

How my ex-girlfriend sees me.

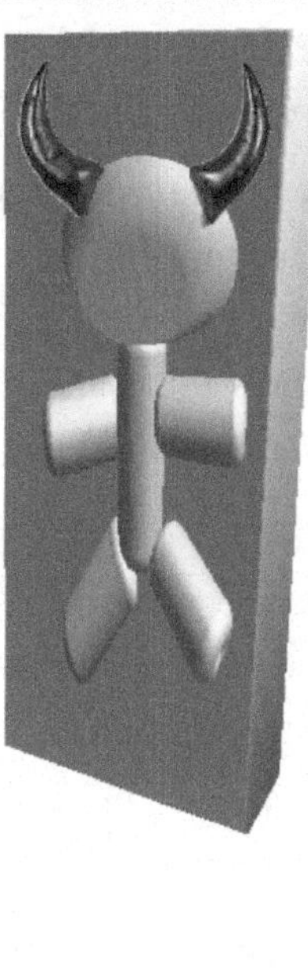

As we age, we engage with this committee and struggle with positive and negative aspects of their influence. We may place people on our committee (often in the process of developing intimacy) only to want them off that committee when we no longer trust them.

We might even get into the very bad habit of either collecting negative and unworthy members to add to our committee (often the case in abuse and trauma situations) or we consider the public in its entirety as an all too influential member (What will the neighbor's think about all this?)

It is my hope that these theories will come into play at different and useful times in our journey through adulthood. I've seen the value of these models as ways of explaining experience and observations that we make of ourselves and others.

To this end, we "stand on the shoulders of giants"… those who came before us and created these most excellent ideas for us to play with. As I stated at the beginning, none of these are complete, none are perfect, but I think they will all be useful. Useful in helping us understand ourselves and each other through adulthood.

Assessment

Chapter 2 Discussion

At the end of this course we will be examining the human experience and the commonly identified human need for meaning. Consider the psychological theories that you have encountered here and in prior courses. Describe if and how any of these may have contributed to you having a deeper understanding of meaning in your life.

Chapter 2 Assignment - Theories

Purpose

The purpose of this assignment is to apply the specifics of select theories of human development to your current understanding of your own development.

You will find that one of the best ways to understand some of these models is to apply them to yourself and the people you know.

Skills and Knowledge

You will demonstrate the following skills and knowledge by completing this assignment:

1. Apply various theories of human development.

Task

In this assignment you will address the following theories. I have made a couple suggestions as to how you might approach each one, but you are not limited to these options.

Erikson's Psychosocial Identity Development

In this section you might consider your most recent and current stages. Maybe describe how you know that you have completed the prior one and what you may be currently working on (in terms of your identity) in your current one.

Identity Status

This theory can be used to track the development of a single aspect of your identity over time. Consider an aspect of your identity that is currently in the "Achievement" status. Write a couple paragraphs outlining the history of this status as it moved from Diffusion, to Moratorium, possibly to Foreclosure, and finally into Achievement.

Cognitive Development

A rich component of this theory is the application of "assimilation" and "accommodation" as it pertains to any aspect of knowledge/schema development. Consider something you have had to learned and describe how you engaged in both assimilation (adding new information) and accommodation (adapting older schemas to fit new data.)

Multiple Intelligence

For this one you can pick either Gardner or Sternberg's models. Simply describe some aspects of your current personality.

Ecology and Looking Glass Self

I find that these two work well together. Your "Looking Glass Self" represents various levels of your ecological/developmental process. Briefly describe the important members of your Looking Glass Self committee and how they have influenced your adult development.

Criteria for Success

Use the rubric below as a guide to this assignment.

Title Page 10 points

Standard title page with name, date, course, college name and the name of the assignment.

Erikson 15 points

Example demonstrates understanding of the theory.

Status 15 points

Example demonstrates understanding of the theory.

Cognition 15 points

Example demonstrates understanding of the theory.

Intelligence 15 points

Example demonstrates understanding of the theory.

Ecology 15 points

Example demonstrates understanding of the theory.

Mechanics 15 points

Spelling, syntax, and organizational structure of the paper. Clear and organized.

Transitions into Adulthood

Attention

The Transformation of Spock

In the Star Trek III - Search for Spock movie, the character Spock has been regenerated from the dead on the Genesis planet. The rapid evolution of the planet speeds up his development and he enters into the state described as **Pon Farr**.

Lt. Savic helps young Spock transition

To make to through this stage, the young Vulcan either has to mate or engage in a ritual battle. Failing to do this leads to a blood fever and death.

Although, in the canon of Star Trek **Pon Farr** happens every seven years, it is definitively portrayed as a transition into adulthood in the Star Trek III movie.

And we thought Jr. High School was tough!

Learning Outcomes

Upon completion of this Chapter, students should be able to:

1. Identify and describe personal experiences as rites of passage.
2. Develop an instrument to measure the adulthood construct in your own culture.

Teaching

Transitions

In the Attention section of this Chapter you were introduced to a ritual within the fantasy universe of Star Trek. Rituals that signify the entrance into adulthood are a part of every culture and we refer to them collectively as **Rites of Passage**.

Cultural anthropologists study cultural rituals in modern and ancient cultures and these particular events are very important in many societies. It is the time where the individual takes on the responsibilities and rights as an adult in the society. In truth, it is the time in which they acquire a new "status" (job title = adult) and new "roles" (job description).

Rites of Passage

When once considers the various rituals and events that occur to usher a person into adulthood, there are some common themes that arise, aspects of all these rituals that seem to be present everywhere.

1. **Rituals** - Specified events and traditions.
2. **Community** - Involvement of others in the family.
3. **Lessons** - Specific things that need to be learned to enter into adulthood.
4. **Challenge** - The person needs to overcome a task that forces them to consider the transition into adulthood seriously.

In the modern world, particularly in the West, there is a definitive absence of these rituals. Events are still there, but each of them competes with the other in a confusing mixed message of when adulthood actually begins.

In many of the rituals described in less technological societies, the rituals are singular and mark a clear transition from childhood into adulthood. Yesterday you were a child and today you are an adult. Many of us may have had events where this experience was had, but they were likely not universal or seen as THE event.

Check out this video that describes the importance of this event and how one family challenged themselves to create a meaningful transition into adulthood for their children.

Personal Experience

While many of us may not be able to clearly identify a specific cultural event where they made the transition into adulthood, there may have been numerous rituals you were a part of that signaled these transitions. I will share my own by way of example, and then I will tell you the first time I really felt like an adult!

The Adulting of Mark Kavanaugh

Confirmation

The first formal ritual I encountered was held within the Catholic Church I was raised in.

MOVIE - An Exploration of Coming of Age

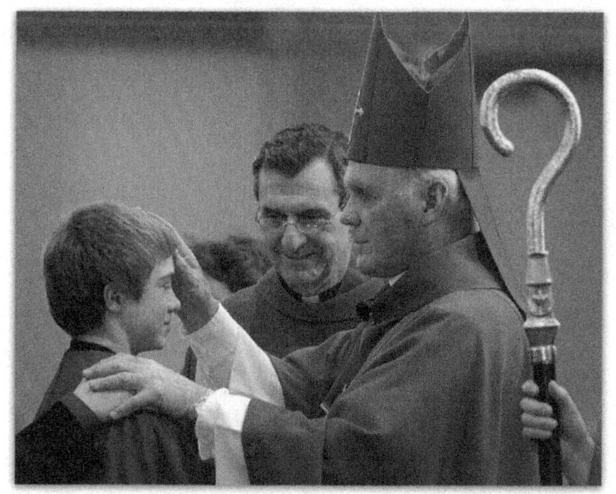

It is the practice of the Sacrament of Confirmation. In the Catholic Church, this is the "official" transformation ceremony when Catholic children become Catholic adults.

This ritual must be seen as an initiation into Catholic Adulthood and a maturity of faith, not so much as ritual into the full responsibilities of being an adult. Yet, it is still a time in which I remember there was something new about me.

Drivers License

I grew up in a small town that was quite isolated. Truth is, I had been driving with friends in the back rural roads for quite some time, but I didn't have my license until will was 16. We all did it. Drivers Education was a class we took in High School. It was the same teacher (Mr. Cyr) and we all looked forward to it.

Passing my driving test and getting my permit was an awesome feeling! I didn't have my own car, but we had an extra one sitting around so I got to use that. It was an AMC Hornet.

We referred to it has the "Brown Hornet" (a play on the same "super hero" character from the cartoon Fat Albert created by Bill Cosby - oh the times have changed!)

18th Birthday

On February 10, 1983 I turned 18. This one is sort of sanctioned by our society because it is our actually age of maturity. I'm legally an adult at this age. This is in no relation to the fact that I was not really acting like an adult or ready for the responsibilities of being an adult. In fact, the message was very mixed because I was still in high school, still a kid, and I was, as the same time, told that I needed to start acting like an adult.

Not so clear! By the way, I couldn't drink alcohol legally yet either so what was the fun in that? (I could but I had to cross the border into Canada where the legal drinking age was 18.)

High School Graduation

So what it is with the robes, the funny hats, the speeches? Something is happening!

This was a big day and there were laughs and tears as we readied ourselves to go on our Project Graduation trip to Quebec City. My mom was a chaperone. This is an important point to make because she is the one who caught me and Andrew at a bar in Quebec. Remember, in Canada, we were 18 and were legal to drink. I guess Andrew and I really never bought into the whole point of "project graduation"!

Despite the deviance, I still felt like I was really moving on…I was going to college and ready to start building my career in Marine Biology.

I wonder how the lack of in-person experience of graduation will impact the memories of graduation in today's COVID-19 society?

College Itself

I will choose to not go into all the experimenting and diverse experiences that I had when I was in college. Let it be known that I am lucky to be alive. This seemed like the testing ground to me. I worked so I always had cash, I was friendly and outgoing, so I had friends, and I was in NY, a short ride from the city that never sleeps!

College Graduation

One would think that having a degree in hand would be the event to launch my adulthood, but I was not ready yet. I left college with a degree in Psychology and headed to central Maine to major in Music at the University of Maine at Augusta.

Not the best choice for a person who had a bit of debt and hearing loss. But I was not known for my great decisions back then.

My First Apartment

When I first moved to Augusta I was living in a room in a house. Great experience but I was not out on my own. When I finally did get my own apartment it really started to sink in. I had to sign a lease, I was 100% responsible for ALL the bills, I had to order electricity and phone service. Wow!

So what even sticks out as to when I **FELT** like an adult? This is a phone book.

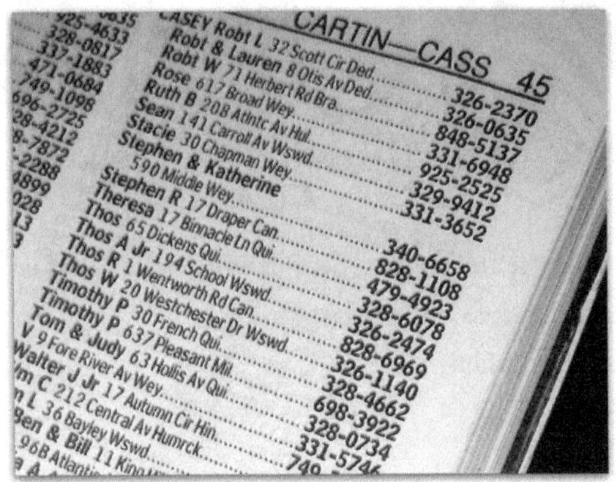

Phonebooks were published periodically by the phone company and sent to all the subscribers. In this new apartment I received my first phone book and looked myself up…and it was ME…not my parents or roommates or anyone else, all me. THAT is when it finally hit me. I'm an adult.

I've been trying to escape ever since!

Things are not Always Clear

You might be able to relate to some of these events. I haven't even included the ones that made me feel MORE like an adult. Specific jobs, having a child, buying a house, etc.

Unlike some of the cultures we learned about earlier in this Chapter, the "day I became an adult" is more personal and, well, in my case, pretty mundane!

As we will see in the next Chapter, in the West we often take on more and more adult-like duties (or we are thrust into them in a sort of rapid Diffusion-type identity development). Our adulthood may not have "happened" as much as it "emerged".

Perhaps it might be of value to explore what it means to be an adult. What does our culture say about the characteristics that make up an adult.

This will be an application of the Social Clock. As we have already covered, the Social Clock identifies what SHOULD be happening at a particular age depending the norms, values, and expectations of that particular culture. So, it is not only the age (status) but also what we are able to do (role).

To explore this aspect of our development I'm going to borrow from the world of Sociology and the world of business!

Let's consider for a moment that you are in desperate need to hire an "Adult" to do the adult things in your life. Before you place your ad, you are going to have to put together a job description.

Job Description of an Adult

Consider the concepts from Sociology that I have already dropped all over this Chapter.

Status - Social status designates the "job title" you have in a particular culture. Depending on the various cultures and groups you belong to, you have a large number of statuses. You are a "student" in this class. You are a "daughter" in your family (you happen to also be a sister, brother, aunt, niece, cousin, etc…that is why families can be so complex!

For this activity, you are looking for someone who has the job title of "Adult".

Role - Role is a term that is often used instead of Status, but they are not the same thing in Sociology. Status is the job title, Role is the job description.

Consider each of the statuses mentioned above. Just in your family you are a "sister"…what is the JOB of a sister? You are also a "daughter"…what is the JOB of a daughter? How about a "cousin" or a "niece"? You see where this is going?

Job Title and Job Description of an Adult

If you had the task, and you will have this task, to develop a job description for an adult, what would it include? What does being an "adult" look like? If you were hiring one to be your adult, what should they be able to do?

Each of us will likely have many items on our list that are common, but others will reflect our own experiences. We might, for instance, all say that adults should "pay their own bills". However, some of you might say that you really have to have "had kids" in order to really be an adult!

These differences reflect the different perspectives we have learned about what it means to be an adult. They are different because although many of us grew up in a similar society, our family cultures are different.

We have a special activity in this Chapter to explore the diversity of our perspectives on being an adult! Each of you will be developing a job description for being an adult!

Assessment

Chapter 3 Discussion

Reflect back upon your own "Rites of Passage". Which ones were significant to you? What is the history of these events in your family? Explore how the expectations for your behavior changed (or didn't change.)

Chapter 3 Assignment - Adult?

Purpose

The purpose of this assignment is to explore the diversity of definitions of "adulthood" held by different people. Adulthood is a socially constructed Status within society with specific expectations for their role(s) in that society. Differences continue to persist among families as to what this really is. These differences create an experience among individuals that makes it difficult to pinpoint when "adulthood" actually happens!

This assignment will explore these differences and determine how well you are doing at being an adult!

Skills and Knowledge

You will demonstrate the following skills and knowledge by completing this assignment:

1. Reflecting cultural norms, values, and expectations related to the status of adulthood.
2. Personal evaluation of performance in this status in relation to your own and others' expectations.

Task

First, I want to be clear that this is an "assignment" but that it will take place in a discussion format. Each of you will be placed in a group (2-3 people) to complete this assignment. The "Discussion" will not be graded, per se, but you will have to post certain documents into your shared Discussion to get a full grade for this assignment. So here are the steps:

1. Each of you are going to come up with a list of 15 characteristics that depict "adulthood". Remember, you are hiring an adult, and this is a test you are going to use to see how "adult" your candidate is.
2. The test will be in the form of a list of characteristics (such as "Pays all their own bills", etc. and a 1-5 scoring for each characteristic. (This is called a Likert Scale and is used very often in Psychology. See below for some additional information.)
3. You will format this test neatly in a document and post a copy of it in the shared Discussion board.
4. The others in your group will do the same.
5. For each of the different "tests" you will rate yourself on your own behaviors as an "adult" over the last 6 months. So you will have to complete your own test and each of the others.
6. Write up a summary of how well you have been doing as an adult over the last sic months. It

will be important for you to give your self a "grade" on each one. The total points available on a 15 item, 5 point likert scale is 75, so your score on each test can range from 0-75. You can convert this to a 0-100 grade using the following formula.

Your Total Points x 100 / 75

Likert Scales

You have seen them all over the place and now you know what they are called. Rating scales are used in all sorts of assessment from personality tests to course evaluations!

A typical Liker Scale that you can use for this assignment is as follows:

1 - Never

2 - Seldom

3 - About half the time

4 - Often

5 - Always

When someone takes your test they will rate themselves on how well they have done on that particular item in the last 6 months. For example, I would give myself a "5" on "Pay my own bills". See the example on the next page for how these can be formatted.

Criteria for Success

Use the rubric below as a guide to this assignment.

Discussion Participation 25 points

You should be an active participant in the discussion with numerous posts.

Initial Blank Test in PDF Format 25 points

Post a copy of your own test for adulthood in PDF format for your peers to use.

Summary 25 points

Post a written summary, not a document, of your results on each of tests that you completed.

Summary Discussion 25 points

Engage in a rich discussion with your peers about the differences between each of the tests and how each other did on each others' tests. You may also explore if some of the items are "fair" or not. This is not a critique of each others' work, it is a sharing of perspective.

Circle the correct numeric response to each question

#	Question	Survey Scale: 1=Strongly Disagree 2=Disagree 3=Neutral 4=Agree 5=Strongly Agree
1	I have easy access to the supplies and equipment I need to do my work on this unit.	1 2 3 4 5
2	The support services to this unit respond in a timely way.	1 2 3 4 5
3	I can discuss challenging issues with care team members on this unit.	1 2 3 4 5
4	My ideas really seem to count on this unit.	1 2 3 4 5

Emerging Adulthood

Attention

A New Stage!

I have been teaching Developmental Psychology at the college level since 1997! I have always enjoyed teaching people about Erikson's stages, but throughout that time there were more and more individuals who were clearly not adolescents anymore, but were really not adults yet...and least not fully.

I'm not prophetic and I'm not as much a researcher to be able to say that I predicted this would happen, but I have long said that there needs to be a stage that come in-between Erikson's 5th and 6th Stage.

so what have you been up to since school?
Mostly I've been trying to figure out why everyone seems so good at being adults while I'm still eating cereal for dinner
/r/honestconversations

Learning Outcomes

Upon completion of this Chapter, students should be able to:

1. Discuss personal experiences with emerging adulthood and adulting.
2. Review a peer-reviewed journal article related to Emerging Adulthood.

Teaching

New Stage

To understand this new stage we need to review Erikson's theory again. We are discussing a stage in-between Stage 5 - Identity vs. Identity Confusion and Stage 6 - Intimacy vs. Isolation. Many of you can probably relate to the very real necessity to create a more solid adult identity prior to taking on the big "intimacy" stage!

Notice that each stage in Erikson's theory is established as a dichotomy. The developmental task is to place oneself on the continuum between these two states with one leaning toward more positive development and the other toward more negative development.

The new stage of Emerging Adulthood covers the area from late teens and across the twenties and is titled

"incarnation vs impudence"

One of the principal researchers and advocated for this new stage has been Jeffrey Jensen Arnett, a Developmental Psychologist at Clark University.

Emerging Adulthood: A Theory of Development from the Late Teens through the Twenties

The above link is the original article my Arnett in May 2000 introducing the notion of Emerging Adulthood. As you can see, it sometimes takes a while for ideas to come to the surface of the world in Psychology and make it mainstream!

Incarnation and Impudence

If we are going to have an understanding of this stage we need to examine these two terms and what they mean in terms of human development.

Incarnation

The stage exists as a protracted time of experimentation with interdependence, independence, dependence, self-sufficiency, and social/sexual/demographic choices. It is not simply an extended adolescence, according to Arnett, because of the social changes that happen in the late teens. They are called into the world of work/college/etc.

To "incarnate" is to accept adult roles and responsibilities, with realistic expectations for the future and concrete plans to achieve those goals.

Impudence

As with all of Erikson's stages, things can go wrong. If the person's experience or choices does not lead to incarnation the individual is said to be impudent.

Impudence is the denial of responsibility, concurrent with the lack of planning, realistic goals, and immodesty.

As I write this definition, I can just imagine that many of you are actually listing the number of individuals you know who are in this state of being!! I have a couple in my own family!

What is Going On?

According to Arnett, this particular stage is characterized by the following:

1. **Age of Identity Exploration** - Young people are deciding who they are and what they want out of school, work, and love. This transitions as individuals discover who they and what they want.

2. **Age of Instability** - The post-high-school years are marked by repeated residence changes, as young people either go to college or live with friends or a romantic partner. For most, frequency moves end as families and careers are established in the 30s. This transitions as they settle down both geographically and in terms of their relationships with others.

3. **Age of Self-Focus** - Free of the parent- and society-directed routine of school, young people try to decide what they want to do, where they want to go, and who they want to be with - before those choices get limited by the constraints of marriage, children, and career. This transitions into making decisions to commit to various aspects of life, particularly in relation to romantic partners. A limiting of choices once options have been explored.

4. **Age of Feeling In-Between** - Many emerging adults say they are taking responsibility for themselves, but do not completely feel like an adult. This transitions with the occurrence of moments where they feel they truly understand adulthood. It may also be accompanied by a realization that their parents are more like peers now than parents.

5. **Age of Possibilities** - Optimism reigns. Most emerging adults believe they have good chances of living "better than their parents did" and even if their parents divorces, they believe they will find a lifelong soulmate. As with self-focus, the commitment to various aspects of their lives limit some choices. The person becomes more focused on their goals and how to achieve them.

Adulting

The term "adulting" has been coined to describe the processes that occur during this period of time. It is both a verb that describes the process and point of joking about the process and challenges that young people face.

One thing to consider is that although the basic challenges of becoming an adult are the same, doing so in a world that is rapidly changing may result in families being less able to provide the kind of instruction and knowledge to make these transitions.

The fact is, a person can be successful in many ways having transitioned to a good job and their own place and yet lack some basic skills such as cooking, cleaning, and maintaining their car.

Individuals in this position may be likely to post statements online about their "accomplishments" such as "cooking their first meal" or "opening their first checking account" that greatly undermine their other accomplishments!

Nonetheless, there is an emerging need for a way for these individuals to acquire these skills. Books and videos about the skills associated with adulting abound. In fact, right here in Portland, Maine, there is a school for adulting that has been featured on National Public Radio

Welcome to the Adulting School

This school features classroom instruction, events, and workshops on all sorts of topics. Check it out!

Assessment

Chapter 4 Discussion

Review the definitions of "Emerging Adulthood" and "Adulting" in this Chapter. Reflect on your own experiences with this content.

Chapter 4 Assignment - Article

Purpose

The purpose of this assignment is to provide an experience in reviewing recent research related to Emerging Adulthood. This will also provide you with the opportunity to work with Library staff to meet the criterial of this assignment.

Skills and Knowledge

You will demonstrate the following skills and knowledge by completing this assignment:

1. Using library staff and resources to locate a recent peer-reviewed journal article related to emerging adulthood.

2. Engage in analytical reading of the peer reviewed article.
3. Summarize the article.
4. Provide a critical analysis of the content of the article and its pragmatic applications.

Task

For this assignment you are going to review a peer-reviewed research article. The article will need to meet two specific criteria.

- The article must come from an issue of the journal "Emerging Adulthood".
- The article must have been published within the last 24 months.

To do this you will likely need to seek the assistance of the library staff. Please do not hesitate to reach out for assistance with this assignment. Finding articles in a specific journal is not a simple task.

Once you have obtained the article you should read it and provide a one-page summary of the findings from the article. This should not be a copy of the abstract, it must be in your own words.

You will then provide a short critical analysis as to the pragmatic use of these findings.

When you submit this assignment, submit the PDF copy of the article as well. There should be two documents that you upload, the article itself and your paper.

Criteria for Success

Use the rubric below as a guide to this assignment.

Title Page 10 points

Standard title page with name, date, course, college name and the name of the assignment.

Article Summary 25 points

Summary outlines the basic design, target population, and results of the article

Applications 25 points

Critical review of the applications of the findings of the article.

Copy of Article 25 points

The article reveals that it meets the criteria set forth in this assignment.

Mechanics 15 points

Spelling, syntax, and organizational structure of the paper. Clear and organized.

Young Adulthood

Attention

Now what?

Now that we have defined Emerging Adulthood, what happens to Young Adulthood? It may be that the creating of a new stage (Emerging) which has characteristics of both Adolescence and Adulthood leaves us with a need to carefully define what we mean by young adulthood.

Sometimes solutions prove to simply create more questions!

Learning Outcomes

Upon completion of this Chapter, students should be able to:

1. Define young adulthood as a distinct stage from Emerging Adulthood.
2. Identify areas of personal identity affirmation.
3. Relate personality test results to decisions made about identity.
4. Discuss examples of Post-Formal Operational thinking.

Teaching

More Adulting

Young Adulthood is the time during which we accumulate the knowledge and experience needed to become experts. We are gaining experience and knowledge in all aspects of our lives: work, play, relationships, economics, politics, and our community.

Specific areas of development that are happening in this stage of life include cognitive changes, identity affirmation, personality affirmation, school/work/career establishment, and intimacy. We will examine school/work/career establishment and intimacy in their own chapters.

Cognitive Development

To this point we have been exploring cognitive development largely within the framework of Piaget's theory. However, Piaget's theory ends with Formal Operational Thinking that develops during adolescence. While the abilities of adolescents to engage in abstract reasoning and rational problem solving are similar to adults, there is still a qualitative difference between the thinking of an adult and that of an adolescent.

Post-Formal Thought

Here is the thing about logic...it does not always work in the real world. Consider this notion that was shown to me when I was learning about adult development.

Problem - There are starving individuals on the interior of the African continent and America has ample food that is rotting away in storage. Why not just give the food to the persons who need it in the world?

On the surface this is logical, but there are lots of complicated logistics associated with getting food from the storage facilities in America to the tables in central Africa:

1. *We need to transport the food across America, the Atlantic Ocean, and then across Africa without the food going bad. Who pays the drivers, the trucks, the gas, etc.*
2. *If we get the food to the shores of Africa, Africa is a huge continent. You can fit three entire continental*

USA maps into a single map of Africa? Roads, gas stations along the way?

3. *Flying the supplies in might work but, again, the land is huge, and where will the land/refuel?*
4. *Flying also assumes that airlines have permission to fly in the airspace of many different countries and territories in the interior.*

Far better to send scientists in there with genetically modified seeds tailored to grow in those areas.

Here are some characteristics of post-formal thinking:

1. Absolutes are rare. Things are rarely all good or all bad or simply right or wrong. Other factors play into these determinations.
2. Simple solutions are rarely the case. Many situations call for complex solutions to complex problems.
3. Subjective factors play a role in the construction of solutions.

Post-formal Operational (PFO) thinking is characterized by a number of factors:

Practicality, Flexibility, and Dialectics

PFO entails the ability to mentally accommodate conflicting perspectives. Dialectical thought, in particular, allows adult thinkers to continually evaluate the pros and cons of a situation.

Adult thinkers can conceptualize a "thesis" or perspective on an idea and then construct an "antithesis" or an opposing perspective. This can be done through the creative process or by incorporating multiple perspectives on an issue into the current **schema**. So, as you can see this is truly a process of "accommodation" and "assimilation" continuing into adult level thinking.

Additional Factors

Another aspect of PFO is the consideration of affective factors. In essence, we have the ability to take emotional and personal factors into consideration. This ties in

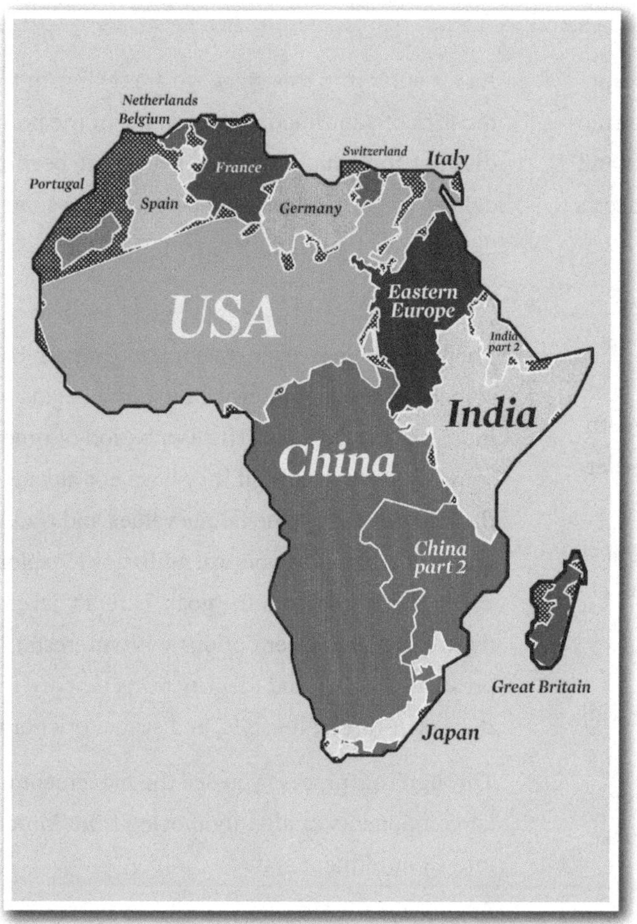

Africa is very big!

Here are a whole lot of other countries that can fit into the land space of Africa quite easily!

the concept of **Emotional Intelligence** to the concept of adult levels of cognition. Our ability to manage emotional content (the emotions and feelings of others and ourselves) when we are engaged in thinking produces a more inclusive perspective.

Yet another aspect of PFO is a depart from absolute truth to relative truth. By this I mean that individual perspectives have the ability to impact what is "true" to that person. This does not mean that individuals with PFO thinking cannot have strong opinions or consider some concept or another to be "true", but they also have the ability to see things relative to others' perspectives and use this ability to test their own **schemas**.

Affirming Identity

Consider once again the model Identity Status. During this phase we are continuing to explore aspects of our identity (Crisis) but more and more of our selves become more firmly in place (Commitment) as we make more and more decisions.

As we enter into this stage we are taking on the characteristics of adulthood and engaging in the process of **individuation** which is to say that we are beginning to define our own culture and personalities somewhat independent of our family.

Moving Out

There is a degree of empowerment that can be felt when someone moves out of the house and begins to take on more responsibilities. This is a period of time where some individuals may, if they have not already, separate themselves from some family values and traditions (such as religion or political affiliation), explore personal goals separate from the goals parents have had for them (aligning career options with interests), and express personality and identity traits that are uniquely their own (dress, lifestyle, and sexual orientation.)

Through this process you see the movement of particular components of identity moving from Moratorium into Commitment status.

Sexual Orientation

Sexual orientation refers to the nature of sexual and romantic attraction. For each of is it defines which sex (or sexes) we are sexually and romantically attracted to. Sexual orientation has been a challenging topic in our society due to the mixture of traditional and religious ideologies in this regard.

The terms that capture most sexual orientation include the following:

1. Heterosexual - attracted to individuals of the opposite sex.
2. Homosexual - attracted to individuals of the same sex.
3. Bisexual - attracted to individuals of both sexes.
4. Asexuality - not attracted to either sexes.

Pansexuality and polysexuality identify individuals who are attracted to a variety of genders and sex types. Not all of these, however, involve sexual orientation. A person, for example, could be "Gender Fluid: Male/Female" but have a "Heterosexual" sexual orientation. It is important to separate the much wider concept of "gender" from "sexual orientation."

As with our experiences with "moving out", many may be coming to terms with their sexuality and are ready to "come out."

Coming Out

It is not uncommon for individuals of non-traditional sexual orientation to keep their status secret. Individuals who realize they are of an alternative sexual orientation may act upon these desires, but keep them very secret in fear of rejection from their family, friends, and community. Some who engage in this behavior are said to be "in the closet", the process of revealing, publicly, one's sexual orientation is referred to as "coming out of the closet" or simply, "coming out."

Coming out can have dramatic repercussions in someone's life. As much as we hear about parents and friends supporting a person's process, we also hear of children kicked out of the house, "excommunicated" from their church, and scorned by their friends.

Affirming Personality

As we age our personalities become more complex and interact considerably with the circumstances we are exposed to. Temperament may be an early indicator of some of the more salient aspects of our personality that remain with us throughout our lives, such as the **Big 5 Traits.**

1. **Openness to Experience** - People who like to learn new things and enjoy new experiences usually score high in openness. Openness includes traits like being insightful and imaginative and having a wide variety of interests.

2. **Conscientiousness** - People that have a high degree of conscientiousness are reliable and prompt. Traits include being organized, methodic, and thorough.

3. **Extroversion** - Extraversion traits include being; energetic, talkative, and assertive (sometime seen as outspoken by Introverts). Extraverts get their energy and drive from others, while introverts are self-driven get their drive from within themselves.

4. **Agreeableness** - As it perhaps sounds, these individuals are warm, friendly, compassionate and cooperative and traits include being kind, affectionate, and sympathetic. In contrast, people with lower levels of agreeableness may be more distant.

5. **Neuroticism** - Neuroticism or Emotional Stability relates to degree of negative emotions. People that score high on neuroticism often experience emotional instability and negative emotions. Characteristics typically include being moody and tense.

Many of you who are taking this course are either emerging or young adults. Up to this time in your life you have likely been firming up aspects of your own personality such as we have been talking about in this Chapter. Consider completing the Big 5 Personality test using the link provided. Are there any aspects of these results that have firmed up to some degree over the course of your young adulthood?

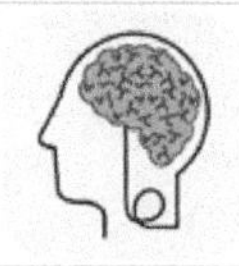

Take the Big 5 Personality Test Online

Assessment

Chapter 5 Discussion

Post-Formal Operational thinking is distinct from the logic of adolescence and developed during Emerging and Young Adulthood. Based on what you have learned about post-formal though, discuss examples of how you have applied these skills in your own life. Be open to make comparisons to how you may have approached these decisions earlier in life.

Chapter 5 Assignment - Affirmations

Purpose

The purpose of this assignment is to explore areas of developmental affirmation related to identity and personality. This assignment will have you reflect upon your development as you experienced moving out, gender/sexual identity, and personality in young adulthood.

Skills and Knowledge

You will demonstrate the following skills and knowledge by completing this assignment:

1. Reflection on affirmation experiences related to young adult development.

Task

For this assignment you are going to reflect on ways in which your identity and personality were affirmed during young adulthood. If some of these aspects of self are still "under development" simply reflect on that.

Consider the following opportunities for affirmative adult development:

- Moving out on your own.
- Gender and sexual orientation identity.
- Personality affirmation

Select two of these and write reflective essays on each one exploring how these components of your self have developed over time and how they "stabilized" during this particular stage in life. If you choose to reflect on personality, do so using the Big 5 personality theory.

Criteria for Success

Use the rubric below as a guide to this assignment.

Title Page — 10 points

Standard title page with name, date, course, college name and the name of the assignment.

Topic #1 — 40 points

Essay outlines content related to the affirmation of one aspect of self.

Topic #2 — 40 points

Essay outlines content related to the affirmation of one aspect of self.

Mechanics — 10 points

Spelling, syntax, and organizational structure of the paper. Clear and organized.

Family, Work, and Education

Attention

Who are you?

Consider for a moment how we introduce ourselves to other people when we meet them. The rituals we go through are designed, in many cases, to convey specific information about ourselves to others. We use this information to shape our interactions with that individual.

Sociologists say that we use this information to judge the person's different statuses and compare them to our own. This shapes our interactions, the topics we are willing to talk about, and our initial first impressions of the person.

Name

One of the first things we might communicate is our name. Not only our first name, which is specific to our individual identity, but also our "last" name which connects us to our "tribe". We have all been in discussions where upon hearing our name we might be asked if we know so-and-so from Montana (someone who shares our last name!)

Gender Status

Often we rely upon visual cues to communicate our gender. All cultures have internal representations for what a particular gender looks and acts like. However, we might include our Mr., Ms. or Mrs. to denote other information or to make it clear what our gender is (and in some cases, our marriage status!)

This is why we might find that individuals with alternative genders tell us about their preferred pronouns. This provides us with critical gender information for our interactions with that person.

Status Symbols

One of the other questions we ask very early on when meeting someone is "What do you do?" What we "do" is such an important aspect of our identity that we spend a great deal of effort and time to develop it, prepare for it and then do it (for years!)

To depict this we might include other titles as we introduce ourselves. Depending on the social situation, I might introduce my self as Dr. Mark Kavanaugh rather than just Mark Kavanaugh. Of course, if I'm doing this at the laundry mat it might be a bit unnecessary!

Other status symbols such as labels, patches, badges, ID tags, and clothing may denote status as well. Some of these are connected to education, high and low status jobs, and authority.

All this happins in just a matter of second when we meet someone for the first time!

Family, Career, and School

These three areas, at least in the US, define a lot of who we are and how others see us. How do we go about making the choices to create these for ourselves?

Learning Outcomes

Upon completion of this Chapter, students should be able to:

1. Discuss family schema.
2. Discuss the development of both career and educational goals in light of results on the Holland test.

Teaching

Family

At this point in the class we are in the traditional Young Adulthood stage of development. After we have transitioned from Emerging Adulthood in Young Adulthood we start to see things "settle down"...and starting a family is one of the most symbolic ways we do this! We often see "settling down" and "starting a family" was inextricably linked.

Family

All of us have one. We all a part of one (traditional or non-traditional), good or bad. We all have an embarrassing uncles somewhere in there! (As my niece and nephew!)

Family is a foundational aspect of our identity and the expectations to start a family of our own may be deeply embedded into our culture. It is an expectation of our family of origin to want a family of our own.

It might even be possible that we want our own family in order to create a better one than the one we are in.

Family is also a natural development of intimacy with others. We will be discussing intimacy in the next Chapter.

Family Schemas

Just like many aspects of our lives we have an internal representation of what "family" means to us and it is a complex, and multifaceted definition. This schema impacts how we set goals to start a family and the expectations we have of how it will come about. Working out our personal definitions of family between ourselves and our partner is an important, if not vital aspect, of creating a successful family.

Prior to this time we may have been too self focused to do this responsibly and take into consideration the expectations of family represented by our partners. This can lead to poor family dynamics, and issues in the family that are difficult to remedy.

Some areas of importance related to our Family Schema include:

- Marriage or co-habitation.
- Children.
- Pets.
- Location.
- Extended family involvement.
- Importance of career.
- Leisure time.
- Friends and past relationships.
- Posssessions.
- Discipline.
- Gender and family roles.
- Sexuality
- Future planning

As you can see, each of these entails some aspect of James Marcia's Identity Status theory. We need to consider our options with each of these and then make decisions in collaboration with our partners.

Career Development

A hallmark of this age is entry into the process of defining one's career. While decisions are sometimes made in Adolescence, the plan (or lack of plan) comes into play in young adulthood. This is also a definitive aspect of our Social Clock, at this age we SHOULD be starting our education or job process in pursuit of our career.

The processes by which we define our career has a very significant impact on our lives. We spend a great deal of time thinking about, preparing for, and engaged in our career. The puzzle pieces associated with career are very important to us. To this end, a number of theories as to how we arrive at "what we do" have been established.

Person-Environment Fit Models

In the early 1900s the prevalent models for career guidance was to seek a match between the environment and personality characteristics of the worker. First we study the individual, then we survey the workplace and match the worker with the workplace.

A good example of this theory is **John Holland's Theory of Career Choice**.

Click here to take a version of the Holland Test

Human Development Models

By the late 1950s, there was a better appreciation of the notion that people changed over time and this concept was applied to how our career changes over time. A good example of this model would be Donald Super's theory. This theory emphasizes the changing roles in our lives and how they relate to our place in the career continuum.

Social Learning Models

Along with other aspects of social learning in the late 1970s, this model builds upon the work of Bandura and the influence our social environment has on our selection of careers. Our unique learning experiences over the course of our lifespan are important determinants of our career choices.

Post Modern Models

This 1980s model focuses mostly on actively processing individual constructs related to self in terms of career identity. Individuals set their sites on a specific career and begin to construct an identity around that career choice.

This is a lot like what goes on with interest inventories, career choice assessments, and career/academic planning in traditional settings.

Life Rainbow

It is important to recognize that the terms in the graphic "growth, exploration, establishment, maintenance, and decline" relate to our self-concept for work and life roles.

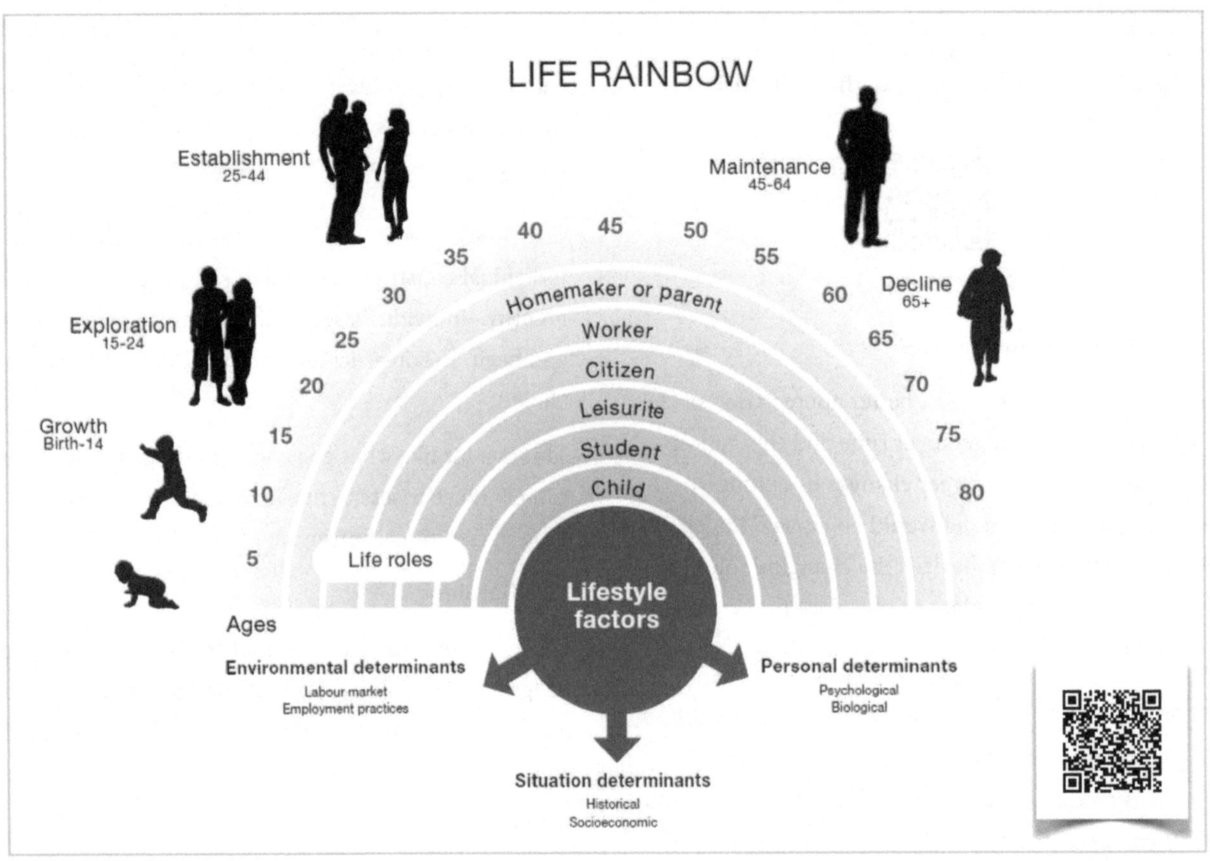

Life Rainbow Graphic

Happenstance

In the 1990s, John Krumboltz conducted research that indicated that chance events in one's life has a tremendous impact on career development.

Many people he interviewed related that the jobs they were in were discovered not so much through planning but through chance conversations and simply "being in the right place at the right time."

However, one needs to prepare the self for the chance events that come along. Some of the characteristics of those open to chance include:

1. Curiosity to explore learning opportunities.
2. Persistence to deal with obstacles.
3. Flexibility to address a variety of circumstances and events.
4. Optimism to maximize benefits from unplanned events.
5. The commitment to ongoing learning and skill development.
6. Ongoing self-assessment.
7. Assessment and feedback from others.
8. Effective networking.
9. Achieving work-life balance.
10. Financial planning to incorporate periods of unemployment.

Education

Finally, we look at our education, which in many ways is closely tied to our Career goals. Different careers may demand specific pathways in education. In addition, we may seek education beyond high school for the challenge of it or simply because it is an expectation in our family culture.

Again, we see the application, at many levels, of Marcia's Identity Status theory. "Crisis" (looking at the options) may be a part of the education process in many ways.

- Education needs based on career.
- Local or away.
- Big school or small school.
- Live in dorm or not.
- Majors and classes at school.
- Clubs, organizations, and activities.
- How far to go in school…college, graduate school, etc.
- Financial choices (cost, financial aid, loans)

Consider your own process of starting school. What choices did you make? Did some aspects of your decision define your decision at the expense of others?

Assessment

Chapter 6 Discussion - Family

Share your original (or current) family schema. Consider the aspects of family listed in the Chapter. Have you had to compromise on any of them.

Chapter 6 Assignment - School/Career

Purpose

In this assignment you will reflect on your own process of deciding on your schooling and career. How did you go about discovering your path (consider the use of Identity Status theory for this.). Did you have to make compromises based on other factors of your life? Did happenstance play any role in your current goals. Take the Holland Test and relate in a post how the test confirms or challenges your current career/education goals.

Skills and Knowledge

You will demonstrate the following skills and knowledge by completing this assignment:

1. Identify the process by which you arrived at your current school/career pathway.
2. Integrate Identity Status theory.
3. Explore the role of happenstance on career development.

Task

For this assignment you are going to write about the process by which you explored and settled upon your current school/career pathway.

Your essay should engage the use of the following:

- Marcia's Identity Status theory - Your essay should outline your journey through the development of your current school/career journey using the concepts of "crisis" and "commitment" and the various statuses from this theory.
- Happenstance - Your essay should explore any chance encounters with individuals or information that played a role in your decision making.
- Holland Test - Your essay should include your current Holland Test scores and a discussion of how they align with your current school/career trajectory.

Criteria for Success

Use the rubric below as a guide to this assignment.

Title Page 10 points

Standard title page with name, date, course, college name and the name of the assignment.

Identity Status 25 points

Essay integrates an understanding of identity status theory.

Happenstance 25 points

Essay integrates an understanding of happenstance.

Holland Codes 25 points

Essay integrates an understanding and understanding of the Holland Codes.

Mechanics 15 points

Spelling, syntax, and organizational structure of the paper. Clear and organized.

Love and Intimacy

7

Attention

Love and Friendship

Love and friendship has been shown to be vital parts of our lives with connections to physical as well as mental health. In the era of COVID distancing this reality has been a significant challenge as we have not had as much opportunity to spend time with those we care about.

We will explore models of relationships with friends, family, and, in many cases, romantic partners. Do we choose our friends and lovers wisely? What impacts these choices? I have a theory of my own about that!

Learning Outcomes

Upon completion of this Chapter, students should be able to:

1. Provide constructive critique to the Puzzle Pieces theory.
2. Contrast the approach to intimacy reflected in both emerging and young adulthood.
3. Utilize Sternberg's Triarchic Theory of Love to describe current relationships.

Teaching

All you need is Love...

John Lennon and Paul McCartney released the song, All you need is Love" in July 1967 as a message to the world that really, Love is all we need...

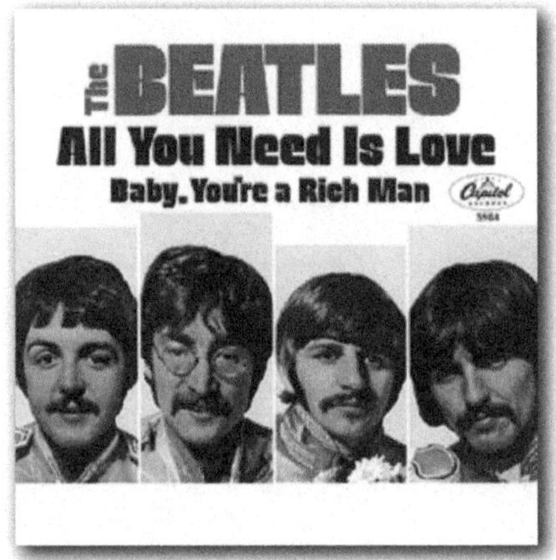

I would never brashly disagree with Lennon on much, but Love (and belonging) is part of a list of things that we need that is outlined beautifully by Abraham Maslow in his famous Hierarchy of Needs.

This will be our first model in our exploration of this vital need in our collective psyche.

Hierarchy of Needs

To understand the place of Love and Belonging we need to understand the way in which Maslow's hierarchy operates. Maslow was one of the first Humanist Psychologist. Humanist Psychology arose out of a frustration with both Psychodynamic (Freud) and Behaviorist perspectives on studying behavior.

Drawing on the early work of the German Gestalt theorists, Humanists felt that the focus of psychological study should:

- Examine the whole person.
- Look at behavior not only through the eyes of the observer, but through the eyes of the person.
- Study the meanings, understandings, and experiences involved in growing teaching and learning.
- Study how people are influenced by their self-perceptions.
- Focus on peoples' responses to internal needs in shaping behavior.

Maslow was a key figure in developing this perspective and his work was wide ranging. He is, though, most famous for his Hierarchy of Needs and his study of Peak Experiences.

Motivation

The theory is basically a theory of motivation. Psychologists are interested in what drives us to do certain things and this theory not only outlines a collection of needs that we seek to satisfy in some way or another, but also an organizational structure that places them in order of priority.

At first, in this history of this theory, Maslow held that each of the needs had to be met in order to move on to the next need in the hierarchy. Later in life, and in his writings, Maslow revised this view and stated that our perceptions of specific needs can override the order they appear in the diagram.

It is important to know that the driving "force" of motivation, the ultimate goal, was no so much for us to move from lower levels of need to higher levels, but that the highest levels of needs we constantly beaconing us to get there. Achieving the highest levels of his theory was the goal, with the lower needs "in the way".

Consider it this way, we are drawn to satisfy lower needs to achieve higher needs...this draw comes from our innate knowledge and need to transcend ourselves.

What draws us to Love?

If we keep this in mind and examine the hierarchy we can contemplate that we are drawn to love by our needs for Esteem and Self-Actualization! In this manner, our respect, self-esteem, status, recognition, strength, and freedom; along with our desire to become more than we can be, are made possible through love. To do this we seek friendship, intimacy, family, and a sense of connection.

Let this remain a continual reminder of why we seek connection with others. Others really embody the mechanism by which we engage in personal growth and ultimately self-actualization.

Before we completely leave Maslow, it is instructive to recognize that while the graphic representation that appears in this book is the one most commonly associated with Maslow's theory, he actually later developed additional Cognitive, Aesthetic (beauty), and Transcendence needs. Keeping to the original triangle shape of the graphic, we see these additional needs in the places they belong in relations to the others.

This expanded model just reinforces the importance of love and belonging on our lives!

Self-actualization
desire to become the most that one can be

Esteem
respect, self-esteem, status, recognition, strength, freedom

Love and belonging
friendship, intimacy, family, sense of connection

Safety needs
personal security, employment, resources, health, property

Physiological needs
air, water, food, shelter, sleep, clothing, reproduction

Intimacy

We recognize that love and belonging are life-long needs that we have and are not situated in any specific time in our lifespan. However, Erikson recognized that the time after adolescence seemed to focus on developing the kind of intimate connections with others that would usher in the generative components of middle adulthood.

In light of our new stage, Emerging Adulthood, we can probably assume that Intimacy (vs. Isolation) is a task that is addressed during both Emerging Adulthood and Young Adulthood. Let's take a look at how these manifest in each stage.

Intimacy in Emerging Adulthood

Consider the components that Arnett stated were descriptive of individuals in emerging adulthood but focus on the specifics of emerging intimacy (I made up THAT term!)

1. **Age of Identity Exploration** - Connecting with others becomes a part of our developing identity. Our statuses change (as we see in Facebook all the time!) from being "single", "in a relationship", to "married" and others. These identities are being considered and explored in emerging adulthood.
2. **Age of Instability** - Relationships are relatively immature. There can be a certain degree of instability and fragile quality to these early relationships.
3. **Age of Self-Focus** - Interestingly, relationships at this point may, depending not eh person, have a focus on utilitarianism. What am I going to get out of this?
4. **Age of Feeling In-Between** - Individuals in remerging adulthood may consider the notions of commitment but might be on the fence, even

though they are living within the expectations of a committed relationship.

5. **Age of Possibilities** - Once characteristic I have seen during this age is a sense of possibilities. Again, depending on the individual, some may be excited about all the possibilities in a relationship but others may be held back by the notion that there may be someone else out there who is "better".

Intimacy in Young Adulthood

We can now explore intimacy as it begins to manifest in the next stage of life, young adulthood. We can define the next stage as the one where there is a "settling down" of the components of intimacy we just reviewed.

1. **Age of Identity Selection** - When we are connected with someone they are incorporated into our identity. Intimacy provides an opportunity to select how this aspect of our identity will play out.
2. **Age of Stability** - Consider that relationships often entail a degree negotiation related to things that will change and things that will not change. This manifests as great degrees of stability in many aspects of the person's life.
3. **Age of Other-Focus** - After an adolescence and emerging adulthood largely focused on the self, now is the time to consider the needs and ambitions of others. This is not to say that people have been selfish, only that the focus has been on personal development.
4. **Age of Feeling Settled** - Many of us have been socialized to consider that finding the people in our lives to meet our intimacy needs will necessitate a sense of completion and settling.
5. **Age of Realities** - Finally we see in this stage a deeper realization of the many realities of living as an adult. Including the compromises and flexibility needed to sustain relationships.

Early Childhood
autonomy vs. shame and doubt

Preschool
initiative vs. guilt

Infancy
trust
vs.
mistrust

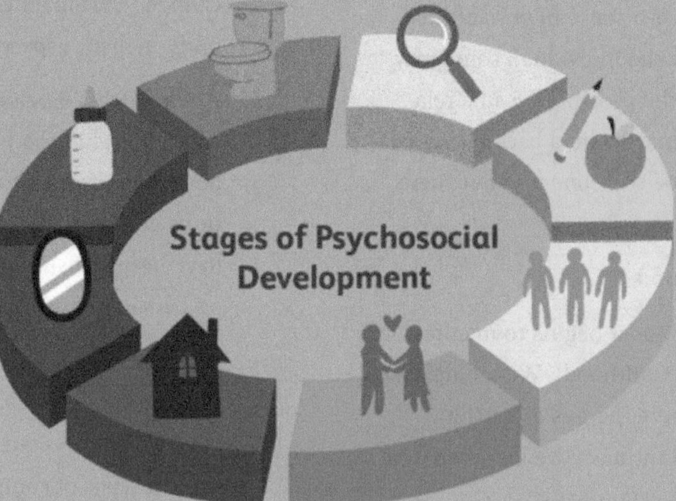

School Age
industry
vs.
inferiority

Maturity
ego integrity
vs.
despair

Adolescence
identity
vs.
role confusion

Middle Adulthood
generativity vs. stagnation

Young Adulthood
intimacy vs. isolation

Erikson's Views

Erikson's theory now turns to the application of one's identity to the tasks of adulthood. Erikson identified that the task of Early Adulthood was the achievement of Intimacy.

We keep in mind that although the word "intimacy" is often associated with "sex", this is not the only application intended by Erikson. His notion of intimacy is inclusive of romantic relationships and sexuality, but it also incorporated deep friendships and connection to community.

Let's remind ourselves of where intimacy lays in the entire context of Erikson's model of psychosocial development. Make some observations as to what Erikson feels needs to be in place BEFORE true intimacy can happen.

Leading up to Intimacy

I find it fascinating to consider what Erikson says needs to be in order for us to move into mature intimacy. According to his theory, we achieve this level of intimacy as a function of our basic trust, our ability to be autonomous (including emotionally), taking initiative, being industrious (specific to the skill set for maintaining good relationships), and finally a fairly solid sense of identity. I pick up on this in my theory of Puzzle Pieces which we will explore later in this Chapter.

Merging Identities

Erikson's perspective on intimacy is that through this process we actually engage in merging out identities with others. Just as we become "other-focused" in our transition out of emerging adulthood, our sense of who we are becomes intertwined with others.

It is difficult to have this sort of conversation without seeming like we are promoting a "loss of self" that is exemplified in the descriptions that we see of "co-dependent" relationships. The fact is, we ARE promoting the idea that mature relationships have dependent qualities about them that need to be separated out from the "over the top" co-dependency versions of them.

Dependency vs. Codependency

Let's examine the features of dependency (D) and codependency (C), and how they differ.

D - Two people rely on each other for love and support and see value in the relationship.

C - One person feels worthless if they are not needed by or making drastic sacrifices for the other.

D - Both make the relationship a priority, but they can still find enjoyment in outside interests, friends, and hobbies.

C - No personal identity, interests, or values outside the codependent relationship.

D - Both can express their emotions and needs and find ways to make the relationship beneficial for both of them.

C - One person believes that their emotions, needs, and desires are not important and will not express them. They may even have a difficult time identifying them.

Attraction

As we make our way toward my Puzzle Pieces theory, we explore what the book has to say about attraction. What draws us to other people in our lives? How do we go about selecting individuals to be our friends? How do we select individuals to pursue romantic relationships with?

1. **Similarity** - First and foremost, we select individuals who share characteristics with us. In

our first social interactions in school, we surrounded ourselves with individuals who shared our same location, age, interests, skills, etc. We connect with others by sharing similar biographies and activities.

2. **Self Disclosure** - As we develop connections with others we establish close friendships with those whom we can share our thoughts without fear of reprisal, with acceptance, and with little risk. Essentially, just as we entered into the world with the task of "Trust vs Mistrust" so we enter into friendships with this analysis.
3. **Proximity** - Although the availability of social media is presenting challenges to this perspective, we largely choose to be friends with those who are in close physical proximity to us. People who live, work, go to school, go to the same church, the same ball games, etc. in our own communities. Proximity has its impact not because we chance upon these individuals when we move about, but because we come in contact with them on a frequent basis.

What are we looking for?

Nearly all of us have asked the question, what are we looking for in a relationship. We know that no one will be ideal (or we are SUPPOSED to know this!) but we do have a list! Maybe a prioritized list.

Many studies have been conducted that attempt to identify what men and women want out of relationships (I would imagine that similar studies are underway to discover the unique desires of persons with other genders so we can stop categorizing them as the "masculine" or "feminine" component of a relationship!). For the time being our knowledge is limited to men and women.

Honesty tops list of traits that people say society values most in men; physical attractiveness top trait for women

What traits or characteristics do you think people in our society ... [OPEN-END]

Value most in men		Value most in women	
33%	Honesty/Morality	35%	Physical attractiveness
23%	Professional/Financial success	30%	Empathy/Nurturing/Kindness
19%	Ambition/Leadership	22%	Intelligence
19%	Strength/Toughness	14%	Honesty/Morality
18%	Hard work/Good work ethic	9%	Ambition/Leadership
11%	Physical attractiveness	9%	Hard work/Good work ethic
11%	Empathy/Nurturing/Kindness	8%	Professional/Financial success
9%	Loyalty/Dependability	7%	Loyalty/Dependability
8%	Intelligence	7%	Competence/Ability
5%	Being family-oriented	6%	Independence/Self-reliance
5%	Politeness/Respectfulness	5%	Strength/Toughness
		5%	Politeness/Respectfulness
		5%	Ability to multitask

Note: Only traits or categories cited by at least 5% of respondents shown. Respondents were allowed to mention up to three traits or characteristics for each question.
Source: Survey of U.S. adults conducted Aug. 8-21 and Sept. 14-28, 2017.
"On Gender Differences, No Consensus on Nature vs. Nurture"

PEW RESEARCH CENTER

Here is some great data from the Pew Research Center. Americans see different Expectations for men and women.

Puzzle Pieces

As I venture into expressing this, as yet, incomplete set of ideas, some historical background is needed.

As a social worker and counselor, I had the occasion to work with many individuals, primarily women, who were involved in what could be easily termed "negative relationships." The characteristics of these relationships varied, but they all had some degree of abuse, neglect, and/or indifference by the husband or boyfriend.

I would add that although my experience of this phenomena has been predominantly with women, I do believe that it exists among men. Men, however, are much less likely to seek help in general, let alone seek help with relationships and admit they are being abused. Some rare studies conducted on male victims abuse seem to indicate that it happens far more often than we may expect.

As a behaviorist, I could not understand why individuals would choose to stay in such negative circumstances. I had learned that "punishment" reduced the behaviors the preceded them, so why would being punished (beaten, neglected, abused) bring about a reduction in "staying in the relationship to make it work" behavior? I was baffled.

Relationship Identity or Personality

Admittedly, I found myself in a similar relationship. That relationship revealed to me the first notion of what was to become Puzzle Pieces. My girlfriend was a sweetheart, caring, giving, supportive, compassionate, and affectionate...when others were around. She was not this way when we were alone. It struck me that she had a particular personality that only revealed itself to me. I was equally not mentally healthy and I had a personality that was only revealed to her. We lived out these personalities to each other alone.

After that relationship ended, and remarkably, we mended fences and built a strong friendship, I began to put the parts together to make up the pieces. Considering the lack of motivation my clients displayed to make change and my own experiences with a unique set of personality characteristics that appeared in my own relationships (I was normally a confident, outgoing person, in relationships I became sensitive, insecure, and extremely possessive and jealous.)

Identity Formation

The first concept I included was the notion of identify formation. As we grow up through Erikson's stages we begin to develop a concept of ourselves. In fact, we develop a concept of multiple aspects of our selves. Some of these are complex collections of traits that make our "work self". Others are sets of characteristics that make up our "friend self". Finally, a specific set of characteristics makes up our "romantic relationship self" These characteristics come about through the experiences we have growing up and we incorporate them into our sense of self when it comes to who we are when we are in relationships.

Attachment

As covered in the book, one of the root characteristics of our relationship identity is formulated through our early attachment experiences. Adults who had specific types of attachment end up with consequential types of adult attachment.

1. Secure Attachment as a child - "I find it relatively easy to get close to others and am comfortable depending on them and having them depend on me. I don't often worry about being abandoned or about someone getting too close to me."
2. Insecure Attachment as a child - "I am somewhat uncomfortable being close to others; I find it difficult to trust them completely , difficult to allow myself to depend on them. I am nervous when anyone gets too close, and often, love partners want me to be more intimate than I feel comfortable being."
3. Anxious/Ambivalent Attachment as a child - "I find that others are reluctant to get as close as I would like. I often worry that my partner doesn't really love me or won't stay with me. I want to merge completely with another person, and this sometimes scares people away."

Parental Role Models

Our first models that teach us about relationships and how we are supposed to behave in them come from our parents. At a young age we are exposed to the type of relationship that our parents have and we accept these as the normal ways in which men and women are supposed to interact. I believe that this becomes our baseline for understanding our own role in relationships and without other confounding experiences, we are likely to be very similar to our same-sex parent in our own relationships.

Happily Ever After

Another early model for relationships occurs in children's stories. I'm not against these stories in any way, but many classic fairy tales not only portray very stringent gender stereotypes (the fair princess needs to be saved by the handsome prince), but they also come to a glorious, happy (every after) ending. One message the sneaks through all of this is that finding a good man, having him sweep you off your feet, and getting married leads to "Happily Ever After."

As adults we know that this is not the way the world really works, but this expectation is embedded into our forming schema of "relationships" long before logic takes a hold. Individuals with strong identities that connect "happiness" with "being in a relationship" will be hypersensitive to ANY threat or imperfection in the relationship. These threats are not only to the couple, but to the persons sense of self.

Television and Media

Early in life we are exposed to television shows (more on this later) and media that both emphasize and trivialize relationships. We are hard pressed to find television shows that do not have a primary "relationship" theme. It seems that it is "all about relationships" and relationships are the most important (and at the same time, least important) aspects of our lives.

This is particularly true in the way in which the media pairs "love" and "sex"...these are practically inseparable in the world of movies and television. Sex is also seen as a solution to relationship problems...who has not seen a television show where an argument ensues, sometimes turning violent, only to be turned into a hot sex scene.

Individuals wedded to this notion will have shallow relationships largely based on physical intimacy. Emotional expression is expressed through sex alone.

Looking at the Next Step

Related to the notion of how relationships and sex are envisioned in the media consider this. Wherever we are in life, we are often living with one foot in the present, and the concerned about what is next. We are a culture of people who plan and prepare for the future. This is a valuable characteristic. If I am in Jr. High I am curious as to what it is like in High School. While I'm in High School, I'm curious about College, etc.

Pre teen children do not necessarily watch television shows that portray the struggles of other pre teens. They are more likely going to look at television shows that show teenagers. The problem with this is, like nearly all of the media, the focus of these shows is often on relationships. A teen is attracted to a girl, a girl and boy are breaking up, etc.

This may have two effects: One, the pre teen gets the notion that being an adolescent is about Intimacy, not Identity. Two, the resolution of these relationships happens readily and quickly in the media...which is not the case in real life. This is a set up for the next influence on the building Relationship Personality.

First Relationships

Even Erikson conceded that despite the focus on identity, romantic relationships begin to happen in adolescence. While this is largely normal it does run some specific risks.

Issue #1 - When adolescent boys and girls of the same age have a relationship, it is well established that the girl is probably much more emotionally and socially mature than the boy. The girl may have very healthy views of the role of relationships, intimacy aside from sexuality, and caring for others. The boy, much less mature, may not be looking for much of that at all. He may be limited to seeking sex and status with his friends. It is easy to tell that makes for some horrible adolescent relationships.

One danger of this type of pairing is that the girl may be convinced that the boy with "love" her if she concedes to have sex with him (he may have even said this.) The fact is, he may say just about anything to get what he wants (check out the lyrics to *Paradise by the Dashboard Light* by Meatloaf.)

She can then be completely crushed when she realizes that his view of "love" after sex was not the same as hers. If they break up, the boy is relatively less impacted and can simply move on, she may be devastated. If we imagine that up to this time she has been bound to him (much like two puzzle pieces fit together) she will be a mess, similar to what would happen if you pulled those pieces apart!

Issue #2 - Erikson states that Identity is the focal point of adolescence. This is true. Imagine that some individuals begin to formulate a sense of themselves that is deeply rooted in who they are with as opposed to who they are. When relationships are happening while identity is forming, it is not impossible to assume that a person's personal identity can be intertwined and incomplete unless they are in a relationship.

As adults, these individuals may find it intolerable to be alone and may only feel complete when they are in a relationship. This goes a long way to explain my early dilemma about why people stay in negative relationships. They may be abused and neglected but at least they are not alone!

Another possibly outcome of this experience is that the woman who longs for the same attachment that she had as a teen will be attracted to men who are immature, need her to survive, and are often addicted. In fact, the teenager who was just in the relationship to have sex is very similar, in personality, to an addict. In my experiences with clients, it was common for the partners to also be addicts.

The Pieces of our Personality

In line with Marcia's Identity Status theory, some of the pieces that make up our Relationship Personality were made for us (Foreclosed), others we made ourselves. This constructivist perspective on our developing personality is the core of Puzzle Pieces. Each of these experiences we have help us shape and build the Relationship Personalty and we actively seek compatible partners.

Sadly, if the Relationship Personality is made up of poor attachment, negative parental role models, unrealistic expectations for happiness, a sense of identity tied to being in a relationship, and negative early relationships...these individuals are prone to have the issues that appeared in my clients. Deeply involved and "stuck" in negative relationships or, conversely, going from one intense, deep relationship with one jerk after another!

Sternberg's Triangular Theory of Love

One of the most balanced psychological definitions of love comes from the work of Robert Sternberg. We were introduced to Sternberg through his Triangular Theory of Intelligence. Sternberg took the same 3-piece philosophy and attempts to define love in a way that is both descriptive (providing definitions for the important parts) and prescriptive (assisting couples in identifying areas in which they can grow.)

Sternberg describes love as being made up of three components: Intimacy, Commitment, and Passion. A

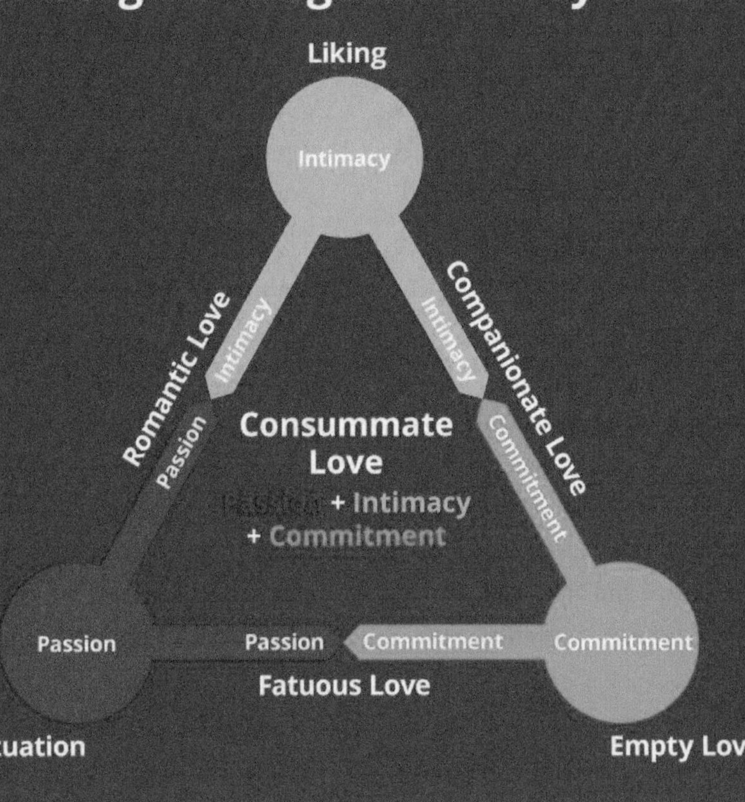

Sternberg's Triangular Theory of Love
Liking
Intimacy
Romantic Love
Intimacy
Passion
Companionate Love
Intimacy
Commitment
Consummate Love
Passion + Intimacy
+ Commitment
Passion
Passion
Commitment
Commitment
Fatuous Love
Infatuation
Empty Love

healthy balance of all of these makes for "consummate love."

Relationships that over-emphasize one or two characteristics earn titles such as "romantic love" and "fatuous love." If a relationship is struggling and one or both partners is unhappy, it is useful to review the need to have all three of these aspects of love together.

The Solutions

Hope is not lost! My model is not simply descriptive but it is also prescriptive. There are things that can be done! If you find that you are in this pattern of relationships, here is what you can do:

1. If you are currently in a negative relationship you may have to seek help to decide if you can stay in the relationship while you make the other changes. This may or may not be possible.
2. If you are currently NOT in a relationship - STAY SINGLE! You have to give yourself some time to focus on the following steps without being tied to your usual habits of wrapping your life around your significant other.
3. Engage in activities that will enhance your personal growth and personal development. Hobbies where you will NOT meet potential partners. Activities that you have "always wanted to do." Reading healthy books, attending groups, exercise, etc. These will help change YOU in ways that will give you confidence and essentially make you "unattractive" and "not attracted" to your traditional jerk. (If you are in a relationship while you do this, you may gradually "grow apart"...this may or may not bring about negative reactions by your partner, above all, he does not want you to change!)
4. When you feel confident that you will not be tempted to go back into the old routine, you can slowly enter the dating world. You may find

that the old type is no longer attractive and they are no longer attracted to you. You may find, instead, that you are attracted to healthier, more nurturing others.

So, here is the "killer" story that drove all this home for me. I met someone who was involved in a series of negative relationships and marriages. She had always ended up in relationships with immature, needy, jobless, alcoholics. When she finally broke free she spent a lot of time with older ladies and went back to school. It was at this point that I met her. She was in the audience at a "singles club" that had invited me to talk about Intimacy from the point of view of Erikson (some of this stuff was under development and I shared it as well.)

She came up to me and described her story as matching what I had talked about. That she had undergone personal growth but that she had to be careful when she was in social situations. She stated that she could walk into a room and almost immediately identify the individuals in the room that were alcoholics. When I asked how she did this, she stated that it was simple...she just identified the ones she was attracted to!

She had figured out that something about her was attracted to this type of person. She made a point of only talking to and engaging with men who she did NOT find attractive. It was through this effort that she found her next relationship. A man who she would have never pictured herself with, but was her perfect match.

Assessment

Chapter 7 Discussion

OK, let me have it! What do you think about the Puzzle Pieces theory and how it addresses issues of long standing negative relationships? Discuss as many details as you wish and it is OK to critique the model as well.

I've been working on it for several years and I'm planning on putting it into book form this Summer.

Chapter 7 Quiz

1. Write an essay that contrasts the approach to intimacy reflected in both emerging and young adulthood.

Chapter 7 Assignment - Relationships

Purpose

The purpose of this assignment is to utilize Sternberg's Triangular Theory of Love to describe different types of relationships in life and to describe the qualities of a specific primary relationship.

Applying the theory in a manner to categorize different people in your life and to examine deep and meaningful relationships is an important component of the application of psychological principles in real life and in the clinical setting.

Skills and Knowledge

You will demonstrate the following skills and knowledge by completing this assignment:

1. Demonstrate an understanding of the application of Sternberg's Triangular Theory of Love.
2. Self reflection on the nature of different relationships in life.
3. Focused reflection on more meaningful and deep relationships in life.

Task

Here is a link to a JPEG version of the Sternberg Theory of Love

Utilize either MS Word or PowerPoint (I would recommend using PowerPoint or Keynote for this assignment.)

Using your preferred application, you will create two pages or slides. Each will contain a copy of the graphic centered in the middle.

The first page/slide will be a description of your different relationships. Using the tapes tool, create boxes or circles with individuals' first names in them and place them on the graphic in the most appropriate place.

The second page/slide will be a detailed score card on how things are going in your current primary relationship. If you are not in a current relationship, you can score a previous relationship. Provide score ratings from 1-10 with 1 being the lowest and 10 being the highest.

This second page/slide is OPTIONAL

Criteria for Success

Use the rubric below as a guide to this assignment.

Title Page/Slide 10 points

Standard title page/slide with name, date, course, college name and the name of the assignment.

Current Relationships (Required) 75 points

This slide/page will contain the graphic with individual's names pasted in the appropriate places.

Primary Relationship (Optional)

This page/slide will provide individual scores from 1-10 on each aspect of the relationship.

Mechanics 15 points

Spelling, syntax, and organizational structure of the paper. Clear and organized.

On the following three pages I have posted an example of each slide including the title slide and the two slides covering the application of Sternberg's theory.

Application of Sternberg's Triangular Theory of Love

Psychology of Adulthood

Mark H. Kavanaugh

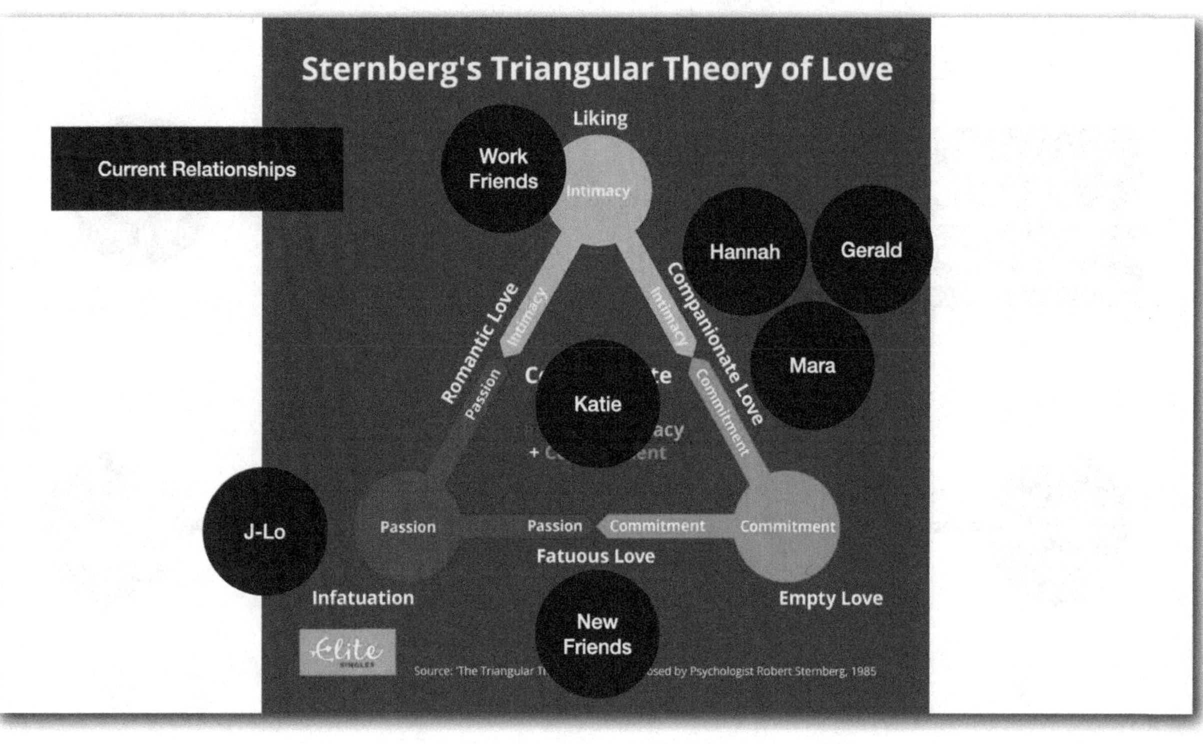
Sternberg's Triangular Theory of Love
Current Relationships
Liking
Work Friends
Intimacy
Hannah
Gerald
Romantic Love
Intimacy
Passion
Companionate Love
Intimacy
Commitment
Mara
Katie
Infatuation
J-Lo
Passion
Passion
Commitment
Commitment
Fatuous Love
Empty Love
New Friends
Elite
Source: 'The Triangular T
osed by Psychologist Robert Sternberg, 1985

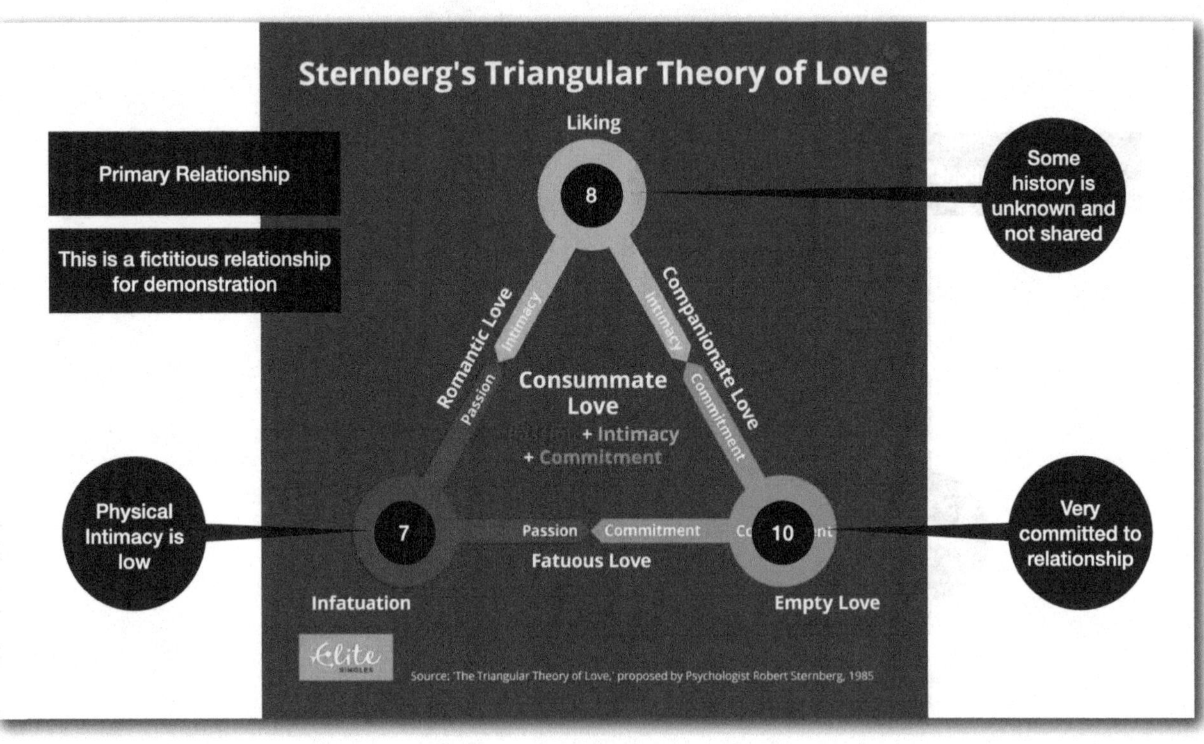
Sternberg's Triangular Theory of Love
Primary Relationship
This is a fictitious relationship for demonstration
Liking
8
Some history is unknown and not shared
Romantic Love
Intimacy
Passion
Companionate Love
Intimacy
Commitment
Consummate Love
+ Intimacy
+ Commitment
Physical Intimacy is low
7
Passion
Commitment
10
Very committed to relationship
Fatuous Love
Infatuation
Empty Love
Elite Singles
Source: 'The Triangular Theory of Love,' proposed by Psychologist Robert Sternberg, 1985

Generativity

Attention

Establishment and Expertise

As I prepared to write this Chapter I found that many of the resources related to the term Generativity referred primarily to the establishment and nurturing of the next generation. On the other hand, I have often thought that this was the stage in which we create our legacy… which may consist of individual accomplishments of different kinds.

There seems to be a continuum of change that occurs from Emerging Adulthood, through Young Adulthood, and into Middle Adulthood. This continuum seems to made up of various activities around establishing, refining, changing, eliminating, replacing, and achieving goals.

At the beginning, goals are very fluid and changing as in the transition between Emerging Adulthood and Young Adulthood. More and more commitments to goals happen throughout Young Adulthood.

At some point we are deep in the process of establishing and accomplishing our goals, which I think might make up the first half of Generativity. Over time we then transition to having expert status in the areas surrounding our goals and in life. We can then be prepared to truly pass on this wisdom to the next generation.

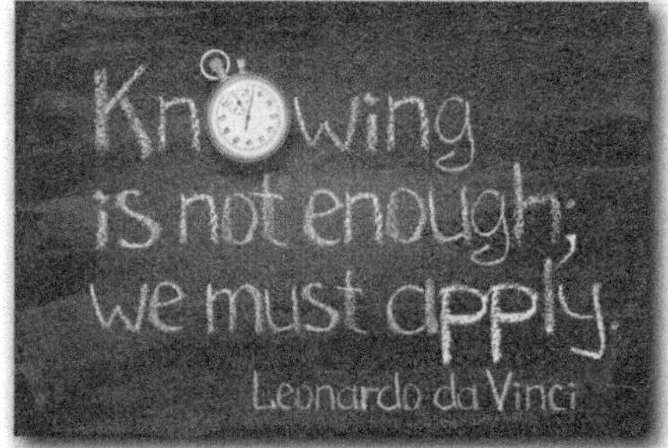

For now we can think of the establishment aspect of this timeframe to be the beginning of Generativity (let's call this Establishment - Early 40s to Early 50s) and the process of leaving a legacy as part of the later half of Generativity (let's call this Expertise - Mid 50s through the 60s).

Learning Outcomes

Upon completion of this Chapter, students should be able to:

1. Discuss personal development of expertise as a pathway to generativity.
2. Present personal reflection regarding the degree of integration between the ideal, social, and real self across the lifespan.

Teaching

Expert Schemas

We have had lots of conversations about the concept of schema. Remember this from our discussion about **assimilation** and **accommodation** and how we construct increasingly complex internal representations of the world.

Over time (and as a result of experience, effort, and learning) some of our schemas become very complex. We become experts at certain things. We are also readily able to identify individuals in our lives who are "expert" at things. Interestingly, Psychology itself struggles with a cohesive perspective on what it means to be an "expert".

What is Expertise?

This article explores various ways in which we define expertise. I'm sure you can find individuals in your own live that you consider to be experts who fit each of these categories.

What is Expertise?

1. Content know-how.
2. Experience and time in a domain.
3. Fluid, automatic behavior, without a whole lot of need to think about it.
4. The use of specific titles such as Dr. or Ph.D.
5. Specific measures such as success, wealth, etc.

In the context of our current study of adulthood, we can see that over time we begin to develop areas of expertise in our own lives.

Practice

According to Malcolm Gladwell, in his book *Outliers*, it takes 10,000 hours (about 10 years) of practice to become an expert at something. Deliberate practice is specifically defined as goal setting, quick feedback, countless drills, etc.

Malcolm Gladwell's *Outliers* on Apple Books

These 10,000 hours might be stretched out over a much longer period of time, so it might take you 20 years to become an expert at something based on this definition.

Consider if there is anything you have done that warrants this kind of label (based on this description).

As we become experts in various things we begin to attract others who see our expertise. We gain confidence in what we are doing and begin to enjoy the opportunity to share what we know with others. This can happen on the job, at home (as a part of parenting), and in our society. You can see that by developing expertise and then being in the position to share it with others we are meeting the needs that arise in Erikson's 7th Stage of Generativity.

Early Expertise - Simone Biles

Expertise can be achieved early in life. We see this with professional athletes and other types of performance artists. Simon Biles is considered by many to be the greatest female gymnast in history. She began gymnastics at age 6, attained a professional coach at age 8, and switched to homeschooling so she could boost her training from 20 hours per week to 35.

She received approximately 7000 hours of training during this homeschooling time well surpassing the 10,000 hours before her Olympic debut, the was 16 when she earned her first World Championship and 4 gold medals at the Rio de Janeiro games in 2016.

Erikson's Generativity

According to Erikson, this is where we make our imprint on the world, where we make our legacy. How do we go about living up to our own expectations? How do we set and attain goals? Why is the so important to us?

As we ask ourselves these questions and consider our own path toward being generative, let's keep in mind that Erikson constructed his stages in dichotomies. If we don't achieve generativity, the other option is **stagnation**.

Stagnation implies a sense of disconnection and unproductively in life. A deep sense of having not taken opportunities and possibly various regrets. In the next Chapter we will be examining a variety of experiences where we confront the direction we are heading in consider new possibilities.

So what are some of the ways in which can achieve generativity? Consider these activities will need to be areas in our lives at which we can become experts (or experts enough) and will formulate a legacy for our lives that we will take into the next stage.

1. **Family** - Creating a family is almost the quintessential example of generativity! Our legacy is in our family, our children, and our home.
2. **Other "Family"** - We can also create a great sense of generativity with our friends and companions. Building lifelong friendships and deep

partnerships can be a very rewarding aspect of our lives.

3. **Work** - We can become experts at whatever it is we do for work. That can provide a deep sense of satisfaction for individuals regardless of the kind of work they do.
4. **Vocation** - I separate out "vocation" from "work" to emphasize that vocation appears to be much more than simply how we use our time. Vocation is the sum total of the work we engage in the has transformative value for us. This may be in our jobs, but it might be in our volunteer or community work.
5. **Creative Efforts** - Certainly some of the most famed examples of generativity are found in the arts. Music, writing, dance, film, etc. Even in the creation of academic contributions, presentations, etc.
6. **Spiritual** - Another way of achieving generativity is through spiritual growth. While this may dove-tail with vocation, family, and other methods, spiritual transformation, transcendence, and peak experiences can lead to a deeply satisfying sense of generativity.

Balancing the Selves

Another process that seems to be associated with this stage of life is an application of the personality theory put forth by Carl Rogers. Carl Rogers was a psychologist most famous for developing concepts in counseling such as "meeting the client what the client is" and "unconditional positive regard". These are concepts that are deeply embedded in current methods of counseling regardless of the different models.

Rogers also develop theory of personality, or rather a theory of our perceptions of our self. His work is known as "Person Centered" and it focused largely on this particular model.

Carl Rogers

The Self

In Roger's definition of the self, he makes several points that include his thoughts about the **experiential field** (the unique sum of our experiences, circumstances, emotions, thoughts, and attitudes), our **self-actualizing tendency** (our motivation to move forward), and our **self**. Rogers felt that by engaging in our experiential field we can have experiences that modify the self and move us toward greater self-actualization. He called this **personal power** and rested it right in the person (as opposed to a doctor.)

The Development of the Personality

When a child is born, it has an innate drive to self-actualize. As a child becomes self aware it develops a need for **positive regard**. If the parents provide **unconditional positive regard** the child will move forward. If the parents, instead, have **conditional positive regard** (positive regard will only be forthcoming under particular circumstances), then the child with develop **conditions of worth**. The child will then begin to act in accordance to these ongoing external demands rather than living his or her own life.

Throughout life, we behave in different ways and evaluate if it is in **congruence** with our perception of our self. We experience **congruence** and we feel good about our behavior when there is a match and we feel **incongruence** when we behave in ways that are not true to our self.

Structure of the Personality

In this section I will be covering Roger's theory of the structure of the self, but I've also added a component to it.

There are, at all times, three versions of the **self** that coexist. These are defined as follows:

1. The **True Self** is the person you really are. This is the one that resides and acts in your unique experiential field. It is the true self that only you know.
2. The **Ideal Self** is the sum of the person you would like to be.
3. The **Social Self** or **Self Image** is the form of the self that you express in public and in society. It is the "you" that everyone else sees.

In one application of Roger's concept of **congruence** we can see this process as an integration of these three selves until they are very similar. The **congruent self** would be the individual who has a true, ideal, and social self that are all the same! In truth, this is very difficult as we strive to be better (ideal self) and we are often in circumstances that call on us to be a different self (social self).

In my experiences I have seen this increased degree of congruence manifest particularly in the elderly population. As we age, we become more aware of our limitations)and may mitigate our ideal self goals) and we become less concerned with what others think about us (social self) so we are just ourselves! Any of you that have elderly relatives that "say it like it is" know exactly what I'm talking about!

The innate drive to self-actualize is sometimes difficult to understand. Western thinking tends to look for tangible answers as to what this means (success, wealth, health, the good life, etc.) Eastern philosophies have been dealing with this concept for much longer and have a very different perspective. To that way of thinking there is a natural order of life, the universe and our place in it.

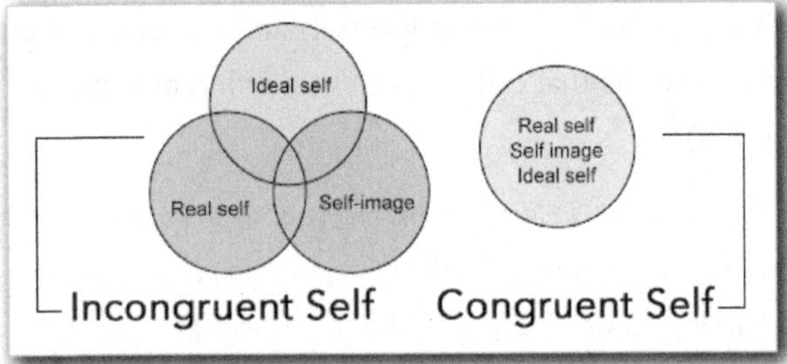

In this image you can see that there is crossover between the different selves in the incongruent self, but total integration of the three selves in the congruent self.

"So whether we believe in God, Tao, an eternal Self, a mortal Self, or merely an actualizing tendency, for thousands of years there has been the belief, amongst many people, that our lives are about more than just being alive for a limited period of time. And it is in the recognition and acceptance, indeed the embracing, of that something more, even if we can't conceive it in our conscious mind, that we find and live a good life."

Assessment

Chapter 8 Discussion

Consider your current areas of expertise and the ones you are attempting to develop through school/work/vocation. Describe how you expect these will contribute to a sense of your on generativity and your opportunity to pass on knowledge and skills to the next generation.

Chapter 8 Assignment - Selves

Purpose

The purpose of this assignment is to apply Roger's Psychology of the Self in a personal analysis of aspects of self that are congruent and non-congruent.

Because this will be submitted as a presentation, this assignment also provides on opportunity to demonstrate oral communication skills.

Skills and Knowledge

You will demonstrate the following skills and knowledge by completing this assignment:

1. Create a slide show with an embedded audio presentation.
2. Demonstrate an understanding of the Roger's Ideal, Self-image, and Real selves.
3. Describe the status of personal congruent and incongruent selves.

Task

Review the content related to Roger's Psychology of the Self. Each of us has aspects of our self that are both congruent and incongruent. Your presentation will focus on describing these aspects of yourself.

You will be submitting a presentation document (slide show) using PowerPoint or Keynote. (Other platforms such as Google Slides have been inconsistent. If you choose to use another tool, you must be sure it is able to export the file so that I can view and hear your presentation.)

To assist with this process I have included some links to resources for how to record narrations across slides in a PowerPoint or Keynote presentation.

The content of the slides is outlined in the Criteria for Success.

Record a Presentation in PowerPoint

Record a Presentation in Keynote

Criteria for Success

Use the rubric below as a guide to this assignment.

Title Page Slide 10 points

Standard title page slide with name, date, course, college name and the name of the assignment.

Description of Theory 35 points

One or more slides accurately portray and describe the Theory of Self.

Application of Theory 40 points

One or more slides accurately provide personal examples of both congruent and incongruent aspects of the self.

Mechanics 15 points

Spelling, syntax, and organizational structure of the paper. Clear and organized.

For this assignment you will need to upload the actual PowerPoint or Keynote file…not a PDF version.

Midlife Events

Attention

Life Begins at 40

On the next page you will find a movie that does a great job capturing the whole concept of midlife. Here is the description of this lecture:

During the 20th century, the midlife crisis became a fashionable means of describing feelings of disillusionment with work, disenchantment with relationships, detachment from family responsibilities, and the growing fear of personal death that began to haunt those beyond the age of forty.

Coined in 1965, the term 'midlife crisis' is often used as satire in popular culture, with numerous examples of stereotypical depictions of rebellion and infidelity. It has been a popular focus of research seeking to explain why and how middle age presents particular social, physiological and emotional challenges.

In this lecture, Professor Mark Jackson, winner of the 2018 Wilkins-Bernal-Medawar Medal, explores a rich range of historical sources to argue that the midlife crisis emerged as a result of demographic changes, new biological accounts of aging, and deepening anxieties about economic decline, political instability, rising level of divorce, and the impact of family breakdown on social cohesion.

LIFE BEGINS AT 40

THE ROYAL SOCIETY

Life Begins at 40 - The Biological and Cultural Roots of the Midlife Crisis

Learning Outcomes

Upon completion of this Chapter, students should be able to:

1. Discuss experiences related to the social expectations associated with midlife crisis.
2. Describe an example of a psychosocial event related to the context of Midlife Crisis.

Teaching

Event vs Crisis

I titled this Chapter Midlife Events rather than Midlife Crisis because I wanted to separate the mystique of "Midlife Crisis" from this conversation for now! Consider this.

Imagine that our life is a road along which we are walking. We have start place/time and we have various destinations along the way, and we have a relatively unknown final destination at the end.

At different point in sour lives we stop and take a step back to look where we are going and figure out if we need to make any course adjustments. From a constructivist point of view, we would be making adjustments to our lives that shape our identity. In essence, we are checking in on the shape of our puzzle pieces and making changes.

Crisis

Recall, once again, the work of Marcia and his definition of Crisis as a process of examining an option. If we are in any moment in our lives where we are examining our current state of being or our trajectory, we are essentially establishing if we need to go into crisis or just continue on our way! There are numerous types of events that can cause us to stop and take account of how we are doing and where we are going.

Psychosocial Events

OK, I'm making up a term again! Psychosocial Events, as I'm going to define here, are the category of events in our lives where we are faced to take stock of our identity. They are not bound to middle of our lives nor are they bound to the factors associated with Midlife Crisis that we will be talking about. Consider the following examples of events that will cause you to refine who you are, get into crisis (to look at your options), and change the direction you are moving in:

1. Graduation.
2. Unexpected pregnancy.
3. Life threatening illness.
4. Loss (family, friend, job, etc.)
5. World events.
6. Opportunity.
7. Spiritual growth.

These can happen at any age and can bring us to the point of reevaluating who we are and where we are going.

Midlife Crisis

I have to admin that I cannot really do much more to explore this topic than the excellent video that can be found in the Attention area of this Chapter.

Here are some brief points I would like to have you look for in this video:

Developmental Clocks

The video does an excellent job of exploring the Developmental Clocks. Psychological and Biological Clocks are most often associated with Midlife Crisis, but the video explores both Social and Historical clocks as well.

New Terms

We have been introduced to some new terms! We all know about Adolescence, but have you ever heard of Middlescence and Senescence? Yeah, me neither! These are useful terms to describe the known factors and transitions that happen during these times.

Midlife Crisis

Keeping an eye on the Psychological and Biological clocks that are still important, we have learned that social/historical changes have produced a sense of the **life cycle**, and expectations associated with what we should have accomplished by certain agers is a strong motivator for us to become anxious about how we are doing.

The entire exploration of the phrase **Life Begins at 40** really sets us up for disappointment if we have chosen to take a rather more meandering path in our lives. Most critical is the notion that the American Dream, associated with a particular pattern of accomplishments including education, work, family, retirement, etc, has now been replaced, in some instances, with a narcissistic pursuit of pleasure and possessions!

When I was watching this video, bells were going off in my head for sure! I have seen this with my own eyes.

Assessment

Chapter 9 Discussion

Discuss your own experiences with social expectations associated with midlife crisis as they are described in the video. Provide examples where you may be caught up in the mystique of Midlife Crisis.

Chapter 9 Quiz

1. Describe in detail a situation that has happened in your life that could be included in the list of Psychosocial Events. Which aspects of your identity, behavior, and other aspects were modified by these events.

Adult Sexuality

Attention

Sex is like Riding a Bike?

Sex, of course, happens across the lifespan. In this sense we are talking about the consensual act of intercourse between two persons.

However, as we age, individuals' thoughts, motivation, and behavior about sex changes. In particular, in older age, persons are less likely to have regular sexual encounters than their younger peers. The reasons for this can be explained by my statement that sex is like riding a bike.

Consider the circumstances under which an older person would or would not ride a bike, and each of these equates to the same reasons why older people may or may not have sex.

They do not own a bike.

As we age we may lose our partners, our social connections, and opportunities for intimacy.

They can't physically ride a bike.

As we age we may have mobility issues that impair our ability to have sex.

We look stupid riding a bike.

Many elderly people may feel shame about their aged bodies and do not wish to be seen naked.

Those who have a bike, can physically ride it, and don't mind looking stupid, ride their bikes!

Learning Outcomes

Upon completion of this Chapter, students should be able to:

1. Reflect on important lessons you have learned regarding sexuality in adulthood.

Teaching

Sex and Relationships

Throughout the lifespan, our closest relationships can support us, comfort us, and provide us with security. Although there is a tendency to either under-emphasize or over-emphasize the importance of sex in relationships, sex is, in the end, may be a very important aspect of a persons' relationships, regardless of age.

In preparation for this Chapter, I did a Google search for the phrase "Sex and Relationships" and got 731,000,000 hits! THIS is your required reading for this Chapter!

In truth, this Chapter is going to focus on topics related to sexuality through adulthood. These include sexual orientation, healthy sexuality, adultery, and riding bicycles.

Sexual Orientation

Any discussion about sexual orientation has to be texted in the larger discussion about gender status. Orientations toward specific anatomy are a part of the collection of social norms we refer to as the genders. However, sexual orientation is also a free variable in the discussion. A person who is biologically male and identifies as a woman can still be either gay, straight, or bisexual. Simply because they identify as a woman does not mean that they are sexually attracted to males.

Why Orientation and not Preference?

In my early experiences with this issue, the term to describe someone's attraction to males or females was "sexual preference". The sad reality, however, is that by referring to this orientation as a "preference" many were able to justify the use of methods that would change a person's preferences (much as in the way our parents would want us to simply "try" the broccoli so KNOW if we like it or not!

Advocacy and politics won the battle to use the term "sexual orientation" in order to remove the "free choice" aspect of the status.

> Personally, I think there is something lost by adopting the term "orientation", not because I think sexuality is always a choice, but because I believe it is sometimes a choice. There are lots of choices that we make through our lives and our choices should be respected regardless of whether they are genetically based.
>
> Just a thought...

Transitions

In earlier Chapters we reviewed the important aspects of development that are associated with identity through adolescence, emerging adulthood, young adulthood, and into middle adulthood. A deeper understanding of emerging sexual orientation can be gained through an application of these same ideas and thoughts.

Although many will attest feeling "different" through childhood, we often see the manifestation of sexual orientation in the teens, at the same time all forms of sexuality begin to emerge. Adolescents may feel themselves attracted to the same or both sexes and may struggle by the messages they receive from the media, family, church, school, and others.

If a teenager feels they are different in a way that brings about a feeling of rejection, this isolation can lead to a number of mental health problems such as depression, truancy, acting out, and suicidal thoughts and actions. Matter-of-fact and open discussions about sexuality at this time are vital, particularly with family members and other important adults.

Planned Parenthood on Sexual Orientation
This website explores definitions and resources for teens and parents.

Emerging and Young Adulthood

Just like other aspects of our identity, we may gingerly step into these statuses and roles through emerging and young adulthood. Through this time, persons may experiment with different identities (crisis) and move toward settling (commitment) on their unique sexuality.

The average of a person "coming out" (going public with friends and family about their sexual orientation) has been going down over the last several decades. LGB individuals who are now in their 60s reveal that they came out at around age 37. It is now significantly lower with gay men coming out at an average of 18, lesbians coming out at 21, and bisexuals coming out at 20.

The Coming Out Experience
Part of a larger survey of LGBT American by the Pew Research Center...a bit dated, 2013, but still very interesting.

Middle Age Crisis

Orientation is an aspect of identity that may become the focus of an individual's midlife event.

Healthy Sexuality

When we consider a healthy, romantic relationship, sexuality or physical intimacy is a very important part of it. You may recall our discussion about Sternberg's Triangular Theory of Love. The part of the diagram related to "Passion" is the one that includes physical intimacy. In this model it is represented as an equal part of the theory with intimacy and commitment.

How this manifests in each relationship is negotiated between the partners in that relationship. Let's explore some of these ideas.

Platonic Relationships

Platonic relationships are those that have no sexual aspect to them at all. This does not mean that there is no physical intimacy. Hugging, holding each other, sleeping together, and hand-holding are all ways in which physical intimacy can manifest in a relationship.

Sex

Sexual behavior happens for the sake of procreation but also for pleasure. Many report that their peak experiences in life have manifest in the sexual encounters with their partners. Questions regarding how often and in what manner partners engage in sex are often a topic in couples counseling.

Ten characteristics of a healthy sexual relationship include:

1. A feeling of well-being.
2. Emotional and physical sensations.
3. Creativity and passion are rediscovered.
4. You nurture yourself in non-genital ways.
5. Suffering and stress are tolerated as part of life.
6. You can be emotionally vulnerable.
7. You develop and maintain healthy boundaries with others.
8. You are curious and caring about others' reactions to you.
9. You learn to trust others.

Notice that this list has a lot to do with your state of mind outside of the actual sex life you have with a partner. Having a healthy sex life means many of these things should be true.

Consent

It is ALWAYS important for sex to be consensual. Being in a committed relationship does not mean that sex happens at any given moment. Both partners should feel the desire to have sex. One of the best lessons I've seen put together regarding consent is the "Consent: Its as simple as Tea" video.

Spice

Either from the beginning or over time, some couples enjoy adding a bit of spice to their romantic encounters.

Consent - Its as Easy as Tea

Feel free to share this video with your entire social network

These might include activities to set the mood, undressing, lingerie, romantic music/food/dancing, etc.

Other couples may be even more adventurous with activities that include experimenting with different positions, sex toys, role playing, and a variety of different locations.

Still others may want to act on the fringe. The popularity of the novels and movies *50 Shades of Gray* revealed at least a passing fascination with such activities such as submissive/dominant relationships, group sex, and open relationships.

The point to be made is that these relationships remain healthy and that people are not exploited.

Adultery

Despite the openness to diverse experience of many partners, adultery (cheating on your partner) remains one of the most destructive behaviors that someone can engage in. For many individuals, a committed relationship, including marriage, implies a promise to remain "faithful" in this manner.

Why People Commit Adultery

Some statistics report that up to 57% of men and 54% of women have reported being unfaithful to their partners at one point or another. The statistics are lower when the individuals are married, 22% and 14% respectively. Marriage does have an impact on the incidence of adultery.

A person may consider and commit adultery for a number of reasons:

- Marital unhappiness
- Boredom/Need for something new
- Revenge
- Narcissism
- Lack of sexual satisfaction
- Falling out of love/In love with another
- Exposure to other cheaters

In nearly every study, a lack of commitment or infidelity is the number one reason for divorce.

The Law

In many states there are adultery laws that make it a crime to have sex when one or both of the parties are married to someone else. This is the case in Alabama, Arizona, Florida, Georgia, Idaho, Illinois, Kansas, Massachusetts, Michigan, Minnesota, Mississippi, New York, North Dakota, Oklahoma, South Carolina, Utah, Virginia, and Wisconsin.

Adultery in the military is actually against the Uniform Code of Military Justice and may be punishable by fines and jail time if processed and proven.

Trust and Betrayal

For many the most destructive aspect of adultery is against trust. An individual that has been the victim of infidelity may develop issues that interfere with their ability to trust others or even engage in romantic relationships again.

While much of the time the relationships that experience this simply end, there is some hope if both partners are willing to work on regaining trust with one another.

Rebuilding the trust in a relationship requires the following:

1. Let yourself be raw with your emotions.
2. Don't ignore what happened.
3. Don't be a helicopter partner.
4. Stay present- and future-oriented.
5. Go to counseling (BOTH OF YOU).
6. Trust yourself.
7. Communicate about communication.

Rebuilding is a task that is best taken on with help and commitment to the process by both individuals.

Riding Bicycles as we Age

At the beginning of this Chapter I discussed the analogy of riding a bike to explain the barriers to sex as we age. According to a study by the AARP and the University of Michigan in 2018, 40% of persons age 65 to 80 are sexually active.

Aging and Human Sexuality Guide by the APA

National Institute on Aging - Sexuality in Later Life

It gets even better...

Many couples indicate a very satisfying sex life late in life. Greater intimacy, fewer distractions, no pregnancy worries, and more time together are some of the reasons why persons in later life may have an even better sex life than they did earlier.

Hormones change...

As we age dips in our hormone levels can impact sexual desire and activity. Vaginal walls get thinner and dryer which can lead to painful intercourse. Menopause and dips in men's testosterone levels impact the ability to have sex.

Battling the hormones...

Using lubricants and vaginal moisturizers may help with dryness and pleasure for her. For men, there is huge market for products to address executive dysfunction (although the actual incidence of ED is much lower than it appears.)

Diabetes...

Diabetes is the disease that just keeps taking things away...including erections in men. Damage to nerve cells and capillaries can lead to ED. Women with diabetes can also lose sensation and are more prone to develop yeast infections.

Heart attack while having sex...

While this might make for interesting television, it is actually very rare. Heart and vascular issues can certainly impact sexuality but when treated, people can still enjoy sex.

Other barriers...

Other medical issues such as weight gain, chronic pain, bladder and bowel control, and the side effects of medication can create barriers.

Getting help...

People of any age should talk to their doctor about concern. There are also therapists who specialize in therapy to find ways to enjoy intimacy and sexuality at any age.

Get creative...

Finding ways to please one another can be a mutual adventure. Toys, different positions, and all the other adventurous things that have already been discussed in this Chapter can open the door to a lasting sex life. Going solo is still an option!

Why bother...

Well, through the lifespan, sex has a lot of benefits:

- Boosts your immune system.
- Burns calories.
- Lowers blood pressure.
- Helps you relax.
- Eases pain.
- Keeps your partner close.

Assessment

Chapter 10 Quiz

1. Consider the content of this Chapter. Reflect on what you have learned and why it is important to you and your career.

Plan B

Attention

Continuity Theory

According to Robert C. Atchley (1989), Continuity Theory of Normal Aging "holds that, in making adaptive choices, middle-aged and older adults attempt to preserve and maintain existing internal and external structures; and they prefer to accomplish this objective by using strategies tied to their past experiences of themselves and their social world. Change is linked to the person's perceived past, producing continuity in inner psychological characteristics as well as in social behavior and in social circumstances. Continuity is thus a grand adaptive strategy that is promoted by both individual preference and social approval."

As we age, we learn ways to adapt to our changing world and we tend to stick with those strategies once they have proven to be "successful". Now, "success" is defined here in the manner that the individual perceives their strategy seems to be successful.

A person who has take on the challenges of life through self-control, continual self-development, and courage will likely approach all challenges in a similar way.

Another person who has taken on the challenges of life through lying, cheating, and alcohol use, will likely approach all challenges in a similar way.

Learning skills related to adult resilience and mental strength early in life allows us to develop very adaptive and forward leaning strategies to address the variety of challenges we face now and in the future.

Atchley, R.C. (1989). A continuity theory of normal aging. The Gerontologist, 29(2), 183-190

Learning Outcomes

Upon completion of this Chapter, students should be able to:

1. Discuss personal experiences with plans that have gone awry and how you made it through.
2. Reflect on the skills associated with resiliency.

Teaching

The best laid plans...

You have likely heard of the phrase "The best laid plans of mice and men often go awry" capturing the impermanence of home and harshness of life. John Steinbeck's famous novel "Of Mice and Men" borrows from the poem "To a Mouse" by Robert Burns. The original line read...

The best laid schemes o' Mice an' Men
Gang aft agley,

I've included the entire poem at the end of the Chapter.

When things go Wrong

Throughout our lives, as I indicated in the Attention section, we tend to approach problems the same way we always have, however that is. Of course, we can learn to approach problems in new ways, but we can predict this continuity of response to new situations.

In many way, something going "wrong" with your plans is an "Identity Crisis" and our friend Marcia comes to our aid again.

Plan A

Just as we effectively go through "crisis" and "commitment" to determine aspects of our identity, we do the same for the PLANS that we have to achieve these identities. We have an Achieved Identity status related to our plans.

		Individual has committed to identity: Yes	Individual has committed to identity: No
Individual has explored identity options	Yes	Identity Achievement	Moratorium
	No	Foreclosure	Identity Diffusion

We can safely say that our PLANS have an achieved identity status because we have explored the options (crisis) and we have committed to a path (commitment).

When circumstances are placed upon us that make our original plans unworkable, we have introduced a "crisis" and we have a few couple choices:

Foreclosure - We can continue, despite circumstances to keep to our original plan and likely experience failure.

Diffusion - We can say "What the hell..." and give up on the idea.

Moratorium - We can begin to look at revising our plans!

Plan B

Now as we begin to explore the process of revising plans, we have to remember that the original plan, particularly if it was well thought out, has a lot of emotional energy behind it and simply moving on to a different plan is often difficult. Consider the incidence of a marriage not working out!

Many people enter into a marriage with the full intent of having it last the rest of their lives. Plan A is to keep the marriage going, and there may be all sorts of other connected plans related to the continuance of that particular relationship.

When that plan fails, it is often a very distressing event because it impacts so many aspects of each person's life. Not only do the basic plans to be married and live together get thrown into crisis, so do many other plans that have been worked out and achieved.

- Living arrangements
- Children
- School
- Career
- Travel
- Savings
- Retirement
- Friends
- Purchases
- Extended family

Grieving for the loss of Plan A can be extensive and life altering. However, faced with challenges, a Plan B must emerge. You can probably easily apply Marcia's model to the various aspects of a failed marriage to see how confused someone's identity can become as achieved components are forced into Foreclosure, Diffusion, and Moratorium.

Planning for Plan B

For certain aspects of our lives, some people like to have a Plan B ready to go, just in case Plan A does not work out. Most college students applied to more than one college when they decided to go back to school. They probably identified a Plan A school and a Plan B school. (Even a C, D, E, and F school!)

When we are applying for jobs, we might want a very specific one, but we may also plan for a second job option. Same when we buy a home, a car, or even have children!

Personally, my mom had a Plan A, B, and C for children. I was the youngest and it took her all the way past my two older brothers to finally get the child she wanted...ME!

Let's consider the identify of a marriage again. With the ease at which divorces can happen, many marriage counselors suggest that the couple develop a **Prenuptial Agreement**.

A Prenuptial Agreement, or a "Prenup", typically lists each persons personal property and which rights each individual will have after the marriage.

While it might seem that persons who engage in this kind of planning are not as committed to the marriage but many marriage counselors disagree.

A Prenup can clarify a number of issues such as:

- Passing property to children of previous relationships.
- Clarifying financial rights.
- Avoiding arguments in case of divorce.
- Protection from debt.

One of the most devastating aspects of a divorce often manifests as continual arguments and disagreements between the two individuals about property. This is particularly harmful for any children that are involved. Anyone that has been involved or familiar with a contentious break up with children involved is probably familiar with how nasty that can get. A prenup can clarify these decisions at a time when the individuals are still treating each other like human beings!

Adult Resilience

For this topic I am relying on the content of a specific book on Adult Resilience.

Reich, J.W., Zaudre, A.J., & Stuart Hall, J. (Eds.). (2010). *Handbook of Adult Resilience.* The Guilford Press, New York.

Resilience can be defined as the capacity one has to adapt to a situation in order to recover from and through them and the capacity to sustain the positive pursuit of goals and happiness despite the experience. Now THAT is a huge definition!

Most of the published work on resilience has focused on children. We wonder how some children who grow up in horrible situations end up so damaged while others seem to continue to thrive despite these challenges. This mysterious capacity that some have to adapt to these circumstances has fascinated psychologist for years.

Much work has also been focused on the mechanisms by which individual recover and come to terms with trauma and other challenges. By our definition, though, this is half the battle. The other aspect of resilience is the return to goals and pursuit of the good life and happiness.

I bring this up in this section of the course because following a disappointing loss or trauma, one may need to arrive at a new plan...Plan B...that will accommodate the emerging realities and allow the person to not only survive the situation they find themselves, but find a path to happiness.

This book is not really a "self-help" text, but one that endeavors to explore the complexity of the human experience through adulthood. To that end, it would be exhaustive to attempt to capture the research and direction the field is going in order to enhance and develop adult resiliency. For our needs, let us list the themes that are present in this work:

Psychobiology matters. We are all armed with certain natural capacities to withstand experiences and adapt to them. Our emotional systems are diverse and we need diverse sets of responses to deal with them. There is no one-size-fits-all solution.

Engaging in **positive emotions** is a building block to adult resilience. Finding joyful things, activities, and nurturing a positive outlook are within our control.

Self-regulation and **emotional intelligence** embody skills that can be learned in therapy, in groups, and even in books.

Recognizing **self-complexity** should be a wonderful experience of self-exploration and discovery. You are complex, and that is OK. It is largely what makes you unique.

When we lose things, regardless of what they are, we must **grieve**. Grieving provides a recognition to the loss, often draws others to you for support, and provides for an emotional release and focus. A bit of depression to pay homage to what has been lost can go a long way.

Faith, **spirituality**, and a **personal cosmology** provides for a larger picture in which your painting (life) resides. Understanding our life in relation to something larger than ourselves places our troubles in perspective. Don't shun "organized religion", it can sometimes be better than "unorganized religion"!

Community with friends, family, and your actual community is essential. We have all been told that humans are social beings. In no way is this more true than in the study of resilience. While we celebrate individual accomplishment in adversity, we must always recognized that these heroes did not operate in a social vacuum.

Resilience and COVID

No social scientist could have predicted the impact that our shared pandemic has had on us. At this writing, we are preparing to go into a Summer that we hope will be full of "back-to-normal" events with a return to the face-to-face classroom experience in the Fall. Yet, we are changed in fundamental ways. When we might say that we will never "return to normal" we might be referring more to our selves rather than our social structure...we will never be the same again.

Many have survived tremendous hurt, pain, and loss through the pandemic. Let alone the experience of being invalidated through social media. Career paths have been altered, learning skills have been put to the test, and many have had to come up with entirely new ways to do things. We had to sustain these changes for a year or more (we are not done!)

Because of the nature of this particular challenge, we have been brought to the awareness of how important social connection is. For many, this has been the most challenging factor of all. Being unable to be in the physical presence of our relatives, friends, and co-workers has made us realize, if we did not know before, how important these relationships are to our sense of self, our identity, our productivity, and even our mental stability.

Perhaps our pre-pandemic "normal" was isolated with an assumption of availability of others. When forced apart, we realize how fleeting that assumption is. Many don't want to return to THAT "normal", but one that is kinder, gentler, and includes more get-togethers, phone calls, and gatherings.

Lesson learned.

Mentally Strong People

I want to finish this Chapter with reference to a work by a friend of mine, Amy Morin. Years ago, Amy was a part-time Faculty at KVCC. She was a Psychotherapist and she taught some Introduction to Psychology classes. As she states on her website, she became an "accidental" author and published a book. She has gone on to publish several others along the same theme and is currently the Editor in Chief of www.verywellmind.com.

Her book is titled *13 Things Mentally Strong People Don't Do.* Her other books include guides to mentally strong parents, women, and children. All on her **website**.

Although a list simplifies what Amy's work covers, it provides an interesting level of insight to how mentally strong people act; how individuals with higher levels of resilience act.

Here are Amy Morin's 13 things that mentally strong (highly resilient) people don't do...

1. Don't waste time feeling sorry for yourself.
2. Don't give away your power.
3. Don't shy away from change.
4. Don't focus on things you can't control.
5. Don't worry about pleasing everyone.
6. Don't fear taking calculated risks.
7. Don't dwell on the past.
8. Don't make the same mistakes over and over.
9. Don't resent other people's success.
10. Don't give up after the first failure.
11. Don't fear alone time.
12. Don't feel the world owes you anything.
13. Don't expect immediate results.

Morin, A. (2014). *13 Things Mentally Strong People Don't Do*. William Morrow.

To a Mouse

As promised, here is the full text of the poem "To a Mouse" by Robert Burns. He wrote this after he accidentally destroyed a mouse's home while farming.

Wee, sleeket, cowran, tim'rous beastie,
O, what a panic's in thy breastie!
Thou need na start awa sae hasty,
    Wi' bickerin brattle!
I wad be laith to rin an' chase thee
    Wi' murd'ring pattle!

I'm truly sorry Man's dominion
Has broken Nature's social union,
An' justifies that ill opinion,

Which makes thee startle,
At me, thy poor, earth-born companion,
An' fellow-mortal!

I doubt na, whyles, but thou may thieve;
What then? poor beastie, thou maun live!
A daimen-icker in a thrave
'S a sma' request:
I'll get a blessin wi' the lave,
An' never miss 't!

Thy wee-bit housie, too, in ruin!
It's silly wa's the win's are strewin!
An' naething, now, to big a new ane,
O' foggage green!
An' bleak December's winds ensuin,
Baith snell an' keen!

Thou saw the fields laid bare an' waste,
An' weary Winter comin fast,
An' cozie here, beneath the blast,
Thou thought to dwell,
Till crash! the cruel coulter past
Out thro' thy cell.

That wee-bit heap o' leaves an' stibble
Has cost thee monie a weary nibble!
Now thou's turn'd out, for a' thy trouble,
But house or hald,
To thole the Winter's sleety dribble,
An' cranreuch cauld!

But Mousie, thou art no thy-lane,
In proving foresight may be vain:
The best laid schemes o' Mice an' Men
Gang aft agley,
An' lea'e us nought but grief an' pain,
For promis'd joy!

Still, thou art blest, compar'd wi' me!
The present only toucheth thee:
But Och! I backward cast my e'e,
On prospects drear!
An' forward tho' I canna see,
I guess an' fear!

Assessment

Chapter 11 Discussion

We have all had plans that have not worked out. Reflect on your own experiences and share how your own activity and the support of others helped you through the situation.

Chapter 11 Assignment - Resilience

Purpose

The purpose of this assignment is to reflect upon the skills and attitudes related to adult resilience. In addition, it is also an opportunity to reflect on activities that one can engage in to develop more resilience.

Skills and Knowledge

You will demonstrate the following skills and knowledge by completing this assignment:

1. Describe personal attributes related to resilience.

2. Evaluate current strengths and needs in these areas.
3. Document a plan to increase personal resilience.

Task

For this assignment you will be examining your personal skills, attributes, and needs across a number of areas related to adult resilience. These areas are those outlined in the Chapter from the **Handbook of Adult Resilience** and Amy Morin's book **13 Things Mentally Strong People Don't Do**.

Your task is to provide a summary of each area that reflects your current skill level, resources, attributes, attitudes, and needs in each one.

Here is the list from the Handbook:

1. Psychobiology
2. Postive Emotions
3. Self-Regulation and Emotional Intelligence
4. Self-Complexity
5. Grieving
6. Faith, Spirituality, and Personal Cosmology
7. Community

Here is Amy Morin's List:

1. Don't waste time feeling sorry for yourself.
2. Don't give away your power.
3. Don't shy away from change.
4. Don't focus on things you can't control.
5. Don't worry about pleasing everyone.
6. Don't fear taking calculated risks.
7. Don't dwell on the past.
8. Don't make the same mistakes over and over.
9. Don't resent other people's success.
10. Don't give up after the first failure.

11. Don't fear alone time.
12. Don't feel the world owes you anything.
13. Don't expect immediate results.

Criteria for Success

Use the rubric below as a guide to this assignment.

Title Page 10 points

Standard title page with name, date, course, college name and the name of the assignment.

Adult Resilience Reflections 25 points

Cover each of the identified areas of skills, attitudes, and resources.

Amy Morin's Reflections 25 points

Evaluate your personal histories, ability, and success in avoiding these behaviors.

Plan 25 points

Develop a plan of action to address areas of deficit and need from the two reflections above.

Mechanics 15 points

Spelling, syntax, and organizational structure of the paper. Clear and organized.

Late Adulthood

Attention

Decline?

Although late adulthood is the age of decline, there are many individuals who live lives in direct contradiction to the stereotypes of the elderly that we hold.

In this chapter, we will explore the typical aspects of aging associated with decline, but we will also examine how important attitude, connection with others, subjective health, and the ability to play throughout the lifespan can dramatically impact a person's experience of aging!

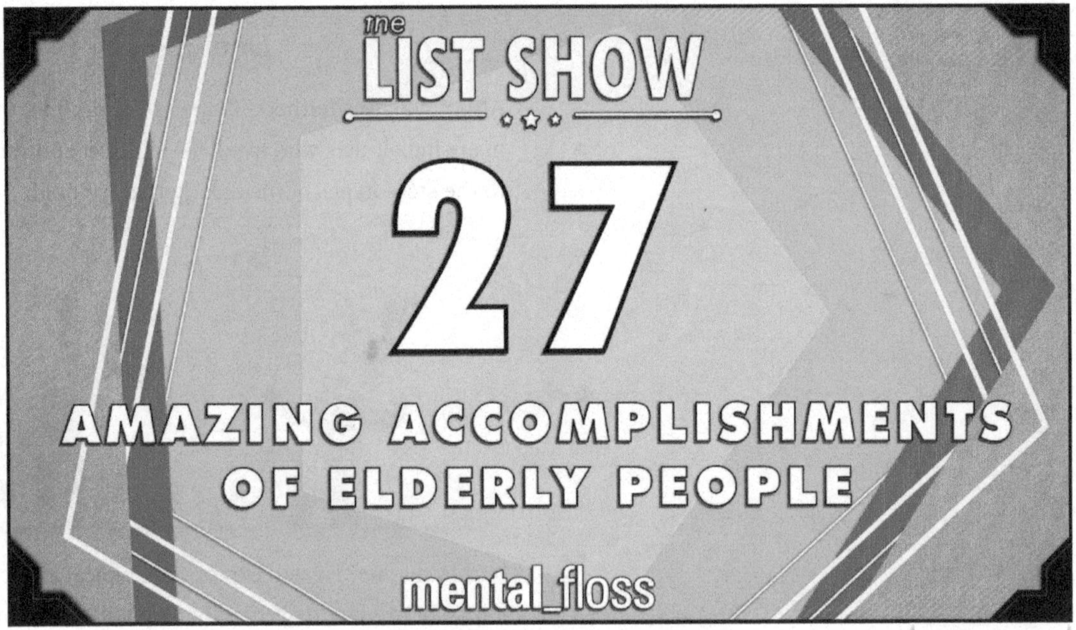

the LIST SHOW

27

AMAZING ACCOMPLISHMENTS OF ELDERLY PEOPLE

mental_floss

MOVIE - 27 Amazing Accomplishments of Elderly People

Learning Outcomes

Upon completion of this Chapter, students should be able to:

1. Discuss the ways in which the advice on aging well combats changes in cognition as we age.

Teaching

The world is getting more gray!

Why gray?

Why do we age? Throughout our lives we replace cells in our bodies with new ones, why don't we keep doing that and live forever?

1. Genetics - it seems that there are certain genes that are responsible for aging and the likelihood of us having a disease. Through the lens of Natural Selection, it is thought that by limiting the lifespan, there is more opportunity for diversity in gene change and mutation in response to environmental changes.

2. Cellular Clock Theory - there are actually two distinct cellular theories, which may combine to determine how we age. According to some research, cells seem to be able to only divide about 40 times. At that point they may simply stop dividing. Related to this is the science around

DNA telomeres. See the movie on the next page!

3. DNA and Mitochondrial Damage - you might remember from Biology class that our cells contain information coded in our DNA and that there is a separate set of DNA in mitochondria. Both of these are subject to damage over time that can cause the cell to lose its ability to convert oxygen into energy using food, and thus they die.

4. Free Radicals - interestingly, when mitochondria produces energy with oxygen they also produce a byproduct of the broken down oxygen called free radicals. Free radicals are unstable molecules that are missing an electron. They tend to take electrons from other molecules and thus damage tissue and cells. While they have the positive impact of destroying bacteria and other harmful organisms in the body, they are also responsible for deteriorating tissue such as skin (wrinkles), eyes (cataracts), nerves (neurodegeneration), vascular tissue (atherosclerosis), and hair follicles (receding hairlines, baldness, and gray hair.)

5. Immune and Hormonal Stress Theories - we have two immune systems in our body, innate and adaptive. The innate system, which includes the skin, mucus membranes and stomach acid, becomes less responsive to defend the body for all the reasons already mentioned. The adaptive immune system, including the tonsils, spleen, thymus, circulatory system, and lymph system, produce "T-cells" which are programmed lymphocytes that attack invaders such as bacteria and viruses. (T-cells are "programmed" by the introduction of vaccines which equip the body to fight off the specific bacteria or virus in question. We attain this new ability when we are

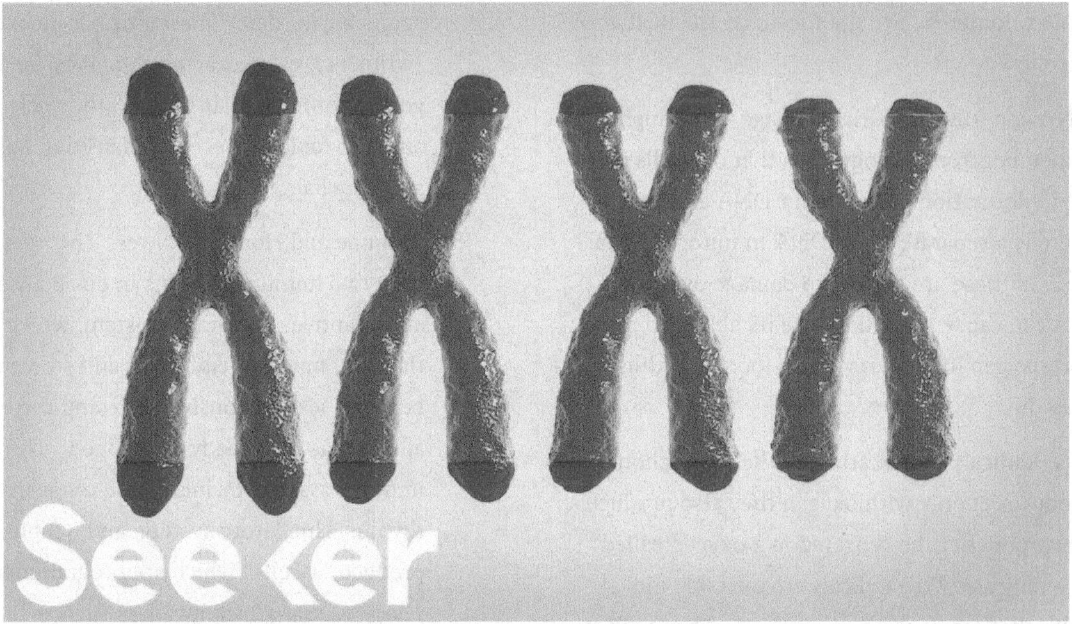

MOVIE - How are your telomeres?

immunized.) Over time we produce fewer T-cells.

6. Neuroendocrine Theory of Aging (Stress) - stress increases the production of cortisol. Excess cortisol damages the hypothalamus and leads to deteriorating conditions such as diabetes, thyroid problems, osteoporosis, and orthostatic hypotension.

Bodily Changes in Aging

1. Tissues lose the amount of water in them, lose elasticity.
2. Skin loses elasticity and becomes thinner.
3. Sarcopenia is the natural loss of muscle tissue due to aging.
4. All the senses reduce in their acuity (smell, taste, vision, touch, hearing)

Life Expectancy

So, how long do you want to live? 75? 80? 120? Forever?

Developmental Psychologists study aging patterns across the globe. How LONG someone lives is called "Longevity" and is determined by genetic and environmental factors.

The Average Life Expectancy is a statistic that determines the age at which 1/2 of the people born in a particular year will be still alive.

The increases in longevity worldwide are due to genetic and environmental factors:

1. Family with a long history of long-lived individuals
2. Low family history of disease
3. Toxins
4. Lifestyle

5. Social class
6. Access to goods and services
7. Access to medical care

Chronic Illness

Because we are living longer, we are more likely to experience one or more chronic illnesses in our lives. In previous generations, the likely cause of death was a sudden onset of an acute illness, such as the flu or tuberculosis. As healthcare got better and more pervasive we have survived these acute illnesses and live long enough to develop the long-term conditions associated with aging.

In addition, the cumulative effect of poor lifestyle choices contributes to the leading causes of death in the world today. Behavioral Medicine is a field of public health that examines and addresses the link between behavior and illness/death.

The differences in life expectancy (women tend to live an average of 5 years longer) between men and women is decreasing since women are more often working outside the home, exposed to the dangers of the workplace, and engaging in the same lifestyle choices as their male counterparts.

Brain Function & Cognitive Processes

What changes in cognitive processing actually do occur as we grow old?

Psychomotor Speed

This is the speed at which we can make a specific response...we might call it "reaction time". People slow down as they get older.

1. May explain other cognitive changes.
2. Decrease in brain white matter which aids in neurological transmission.

Memory

We have all heard the phrase "I'm having an Alzheimer's moment"...but do all old people lose their memory?

To understand the answer to this question, we need to review the different kinds of memory:

1. Episodic Memory---memory of specific events in time (this seems to decline)
2. Semantic Memory---remembering meanings of words and concepts (does not seem to decline)
3. Autobiographical Memory---memory of events during one's life
    1. People remember more vivid memories from their own lives when they were 10-30 years old than when they were older
    2. Less details in the older folks' memories

Concern about memory loss in the elderly has more to do with how that memory loss impacts functioning and anxiety. Having memory aids can help a person function better with memory loss

1. External aids are environmental such as notebooks and calendars.
2. Internal aids rely on mental processes such as imagery.

Mental Health

A great source for all things aging and mental health.

National Council on Aging

Depression

A common misconception is that most, if not all, elderly people are depressed. The fact is, among the healthy population, the rate of clinical depression declines over time.

Older people, however, are faced with a number of potentially "depressing" facts...decline in their activity, change in work and societal value, friends and family dying, poverty, illness, disability, impending death...it is not surprising that we ASSUME that to be old is to be depressed!

Dementia and Alzheimer’s

Dementia is the term for a class of disorders that impact behavior and cognitive functioning. The most famous of these is Alzheimer's Disease.

Key symptoms of Alzheimer's Disease include the following:

1. gradual decline in memory. learning, attention, and judgment
2. difficulty in communicating (often searching for the right word...)
3. decline in personal hygiene and self-care skills
4. changes in behavior and personality

The definitive diagnosis of Alzheimer's can only be made upon examination of the brain after the person has died.

However, there are some warning signs.

Warning Signs

Note: This list is for information only and not a substitute for a consultation with a qualified professional.

1. Memory loss that disrupts daily life. One of the most common signs of Alzheimer’s, especially in the early stages, is forgetting recently learned information. Others include forgetting important

dates or events; asking for the same information over and over; relying on memory aides (e.g., reminder notes or electronic devices) or family members for things they used to handle on their own. What's typical? Sometimes forgetting names or appointments, but remembering them later.

2. Challenges in planning or solving problems. Some people may experience changes in their ability to develop and follow a plan or work with numbers. They may have trouble following a familiar recipe or keeping track of monthly bills. They may have difficulty concentrating and take much longer to do things than they did before. What's typical? Making occasional errors when balancing a checkbook.

3. Difficulty completing familiar tasks at home, at work or at leisure. People with Alzheimer's often find it hard to complete daily tasks. Sometimes, people may have trouble driving to a familiar location, managing a budget at work or remembering the rules of a favorite game. What's typical? Occasionally needing help to use the settings on a microwave or to record a television show.

4. Confusion with time or place. People with Alzheimer's can lose track of dates, seasons and the passage of time. They may have trouble understanding something if it is not happening immediately. Sometimes they may forget where they are or how they got there. What's typical? Getting confused about the day of the week but figuring it out later.

5. Trouble understanding visual images and spatial relationships. For some people, having vision problems is a sign of Alzheimer's. They may have difficulty reading, judging distance and determining color or contrast. In terms of percep-

tion, they may pass a mirror and think someone else is in the room. They may not recognize their own reflection. What's typical? Vision changes related to cataracts.

6. New problems with words in speaking or writing. People with Alzheimer's may have trouble following or joining a conversation. They may stop in the middle of a conversation and have no idea how to continue or they may repeat themselves. They may struggle with vocabulary, have problems finding the right word or call things by the wrong name (e.g., calling a watch a "hand clock"). What's typical? Sometimes having trouble finding the right word.

7. Misplacing things and losing the ability to retrace steps. A person with Alzheimer's disease may put things in unusual places. They may lose things and be unable to go back over their steps to find them again. Sometimes, they may accuse others of stealing. This may occur more frequently over time. What's typical? Misplacing things from time to time, such as a pair of glasses or the remote control.

8. Decreased or poor judgment. People with Alzheimer's may experience changes in judgment or decision making. For example, they may use poor judgment when dealing with money, giving large amounts to telemarketers. They may pay less attention to grooming or keeping themselves clean. What's typical? Making a bad decision once in a while.

9. Withdrawal from work or social activities. A person with Alzheimer's may start to remove themselves from hobbies, social activities, work projects or sports. They may have trouble keeping up with a favorite sports team or remembering how to complete a favorite hobby. They may also avoid being social because of the changes

they have experienced. What's typical? Sometimes feeling weary of work, family and social obligations.

10. Changes in mood and personality. The mood and personalities of people with Alzheimer's can change. They can become confused, suspicious, depressed, fearful or anxious. They may be easily upset at home, at work, with friends or in places where they are out of their comfort zone. What's typical? Developing very specific ways of doing things and becoming irritable when a routine is disrupted.

If you have questions about any of these warning signs, the Alzheimer's Association recommends consulting a physician. Early diagnosis provides the best opportunities for treatment, support and future planning.

Brain Changes Associated with Dementia

Changes in cognition and memory as we age cannot be separated from the neurological changes that occur during this time.

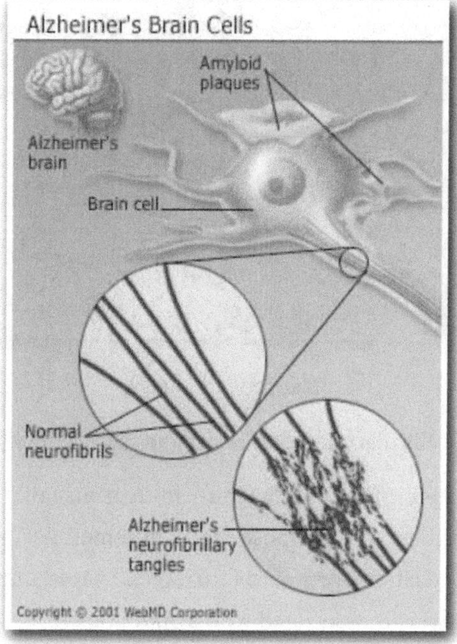

Here are some change that occur on the neurological/ brain level as we age:

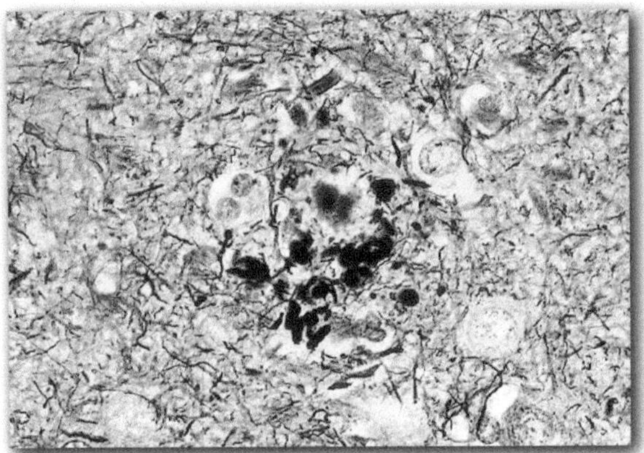

Neuretic Plaques

Neurofibrillary Tangles associated with Alzheimer's

1. Neurofibrillary Tangles---for reasons unknown, fibers that compose the axon sometimes become twisted together to form spiral shaped masses (this is associated with symptoms of Alzheimer's Disease)
2. Neuretic Plaques---damaged and dying neurons sometimes collect around a core of protein
3. Reduced levels of neurotransmitters

The Nun Study

Information about the Nun Study can be found by clicking here. Take time to review the F.A.Q., Videos, and Publications sections of this website.

According to the website...

The Nun Study is a longitudinal study of aging and Alzheimer's disease. It began in 1986 as a pilot study on aging and disability using data collected from the older School Sisters of Notre Dame living in Mankato, Minn. In 1990, the Nun Study was expanded to include older Notre Dames living in the midwestern, eastern, and southern regions of the United States. In 2008 the study returned to the University of Minnesota under the direction of Kelvin O. Lim, M.D. The goal of the Nun Study is to determine the causes and prevention of

Alzheimer's disease, other brain diseases, and the mental and physical disability associated with old age.

The results from these studies can be found in the "Publications" section of this website. Review the "Nun Study Abstracts (with references) document. This is very scientific stuff so be prepared!

The Nun Study

Aging Well

Consider the following list of findings from the Vaillant study at Harvard University:

1. It is not the bad things that happen to us that doom us; it is the good people that happen to us at any age that facilitate enjoyable old age.
2. Healing relationships are facilitated by a capacity for gratitude, for forgiveness, and for taking people inside.
3. A good marriage at age 50 predicted positive aging at 80. But, surprisingly, low cholesterol at 50 did not.
4. Alcohol abuse - unrelated to unhappy childhood - consistently predicted unsuccessful aging, in part because alcoholism damaged future social supports.
5. Learning to play and create after retirement and learning to gain younger friends as we lose older ones adds more to life's enjoyment than retirement income.
6. Objective good physical health was less important to successful aging than was subjective health.

Psychosocial health contrasts the Happy-Well (Integrated) person with the Sad-Sick (Despair) person. One has to consider, however, that there are many ways in which a person can be "sick". This is psychosocial sickness...

1. attitudes
2. depression
3. motivation
4. emotions
5. friends

Consider the six dimensions used to differentiate between the Happy-Well (Integrated) and the Sad-Sick (Despair)person:

1. Absence of objective physical disability
2. Subjective physical health
3. Length of non-disabled life
4. Objective mental health
5. Objective social supports
6. Subjective life satisfaction

Successful Lifespan Development

"A test of successful living, then, becomes learning to live with neither too much desire and adventure nor too much caution and self-care." (Vaillant, p. 61)

As we age we may begin to cope better with our lives and our emotions. Our dysfunctional coping mechanisms may include:

1. Projection
2. Passive aggression
3. Dissociation
4. Acting out
5. Fantasy

More functional tools may include:

1. Sublimation (turning a negative into a positive)

2. Humor
3. Altruism
4. Suppression (often seen as a negative, suppression postpones memories, and even according to Freud, was a "hallmark of maturity")

Summary

So...how do we sum up all of what we have learned about successful aging? I like what Vaillant does in the beginning of Chapter 12 when he refers to old age AA watchwords:

1. Let go and let God
2. First things first
3. Keep it simple
4. Carpe diem
5. Use the telephone

References

Vaillant, G.E. (2002). Aging Well: Guideposts to a Happier Life. New York: Little, Brown and Company.

Assessment

Chapter 12 Discussion

Review the information on aging well and discuss how these methods may address the cognitive changes that occur while we age.

Discuss ways in which you are practicing these strategies to remain sharp as you age.

Changing Roles

13

Attention

Role of the Elderly Through History

Across different cultures the role of the senior citizen has changed dramatically. Visit this site and explore this fascinating topic.

Role of Senior Citizens

Learning Outcomes

Upon completion of this Chapter, students should be able to:

1. Reflect on the value of elderly people in your own life as sources of wisdom.

Teaching

Psychosocial Development

Integrity vs. Despair

Here we are in Erikson's last stage of the lifespan. In this stage people take on the task of weaving together the threads of their lives and putting them all together into a unified sense of self (integrity) to fail to do so is to have extreme regrets and sorrows of past opportunities and decisions (despair).

People can achieve Integrity and continued Generativity in late life:

1. Volunteers
2. Grand Parents
3. Social Networks
4. Consulting

One of the characteristic tasks to accomplish during this stage is to weave together one's life story into an interconnected "tapestry" of meaning. This "life review"

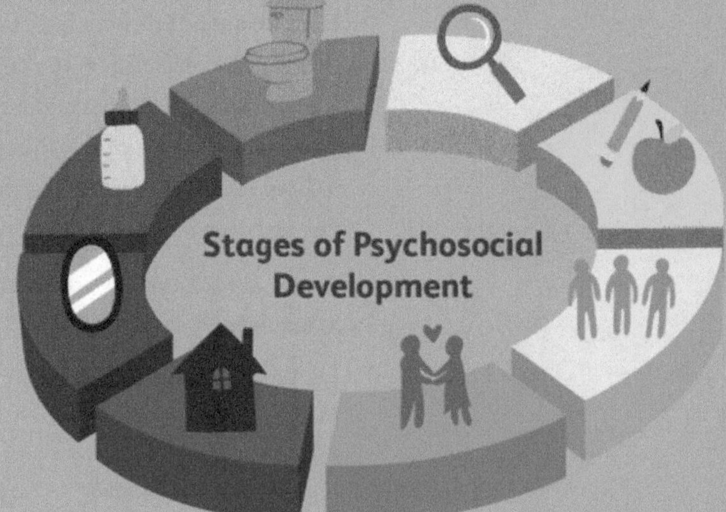
Early Childhood
autonomy vs. shame and doubt
Preschool
initiative vs. guilt
Infancy
trust
vs.
mistrust
School Age
industry
vs.
inferiority
Stages of Psychosocial
Development
Maturity
ego integrity
vs.
despair
Adolescence
identity
vs.
role confusion
Middle Adulthood
generativity vs. stagnation
Young Adulthood
intimacy vs. isolation

process is common among the elderly as they often enjoy relating stories of their lives and the way things "used to be."

Change of Identity

Retirement means a change in identity...occupational identity, but this is a very important part of our selves. For many the transition is gradual...some might continue working part time, work another "bridge job", or may not be able to fully retire due to financial need.

For some, retirement is a time to return to generativity...volunteering, projects, helping others, leadership in civic organizations, hobbies, etc.

Work

One of the major transitions we experience is leaving work...remember how important work has been in shaping our identity (whether that work has been in a business or raising a family) our role and status is changing.

Up until the 1930s, when the railroad union promoted a bill to mandate retirement and when Social Security was inaugurated (1935) most people did not think of retiring. (The life expectancy at that time was 65...so it was presumed that only half of the people who would become eligible to collect Social Security would actually live long enough to get it!)

What about now? Certainly the generation that is about to retire (Baby Boomers) are ready...but does the next generation expect to retire?

Friends and Siblings

Interestingly, through this transition, friends and siblings (rather than children) become increasingly important.

These changes can be a challenge for marriage partners as well.

Understanding Aging

Growing old fills many people with a sense of dread and fear. Some people don't even like to be around older people. The number of psychologists studying child development is a LOT higher than the number of people studying old age...even though we spend a LOT more time in old age than we do in childhood!

Creative Output

Overall, creative output tends to increase through the 30's, peak in the early 40's, and decline thereafter...though there are ample examples of individuals who are creative late in life.

Wisdom

What does it mean to be wise? Her are four characteristics of wisdom:

1. Wisdom deals with important or difficult matters of life and the human condition.
2. Wisdom is truly "superior" knowledge, judgment, and advice.
3. Wisdom is knowledge with extraordinary scope, depth, and balance that is applicable to specific situations.
4. Wisdom, when used, is well intended and combines mind and virtue.

The Wagon Wheel by Dr. Robert Veon

How do we see Aging? This is what the large wagon wheel reclining against the old birch in the white snow teaches us by its simple beauty. No one of its spokes is more important limn the others, but together they make the circle full and reveal the hub as the core of its strength. The more we look at it, the more we come to realize that we have only one life cycle to live, and that living it is the source of our greatest joy.

The restful accomplishment of the old wheel tells us the story of life. Entering into the world we arc what we a.re given, and for many years thereafter parents and grandparents , brothers and sister,. friends and lovers keep giving to us - some more, some less, some hesitantly, some generously. When we finally stand on our own two feet, speak our own wonts, and express our own unique self in work and love, we realize how much is given to us. But wMlc reaching the height of our cycle, and saying with a sense of confidence, "I really am," we sense that to fulfill our life we now arc called to become parents and grandparents, brothers and sisters, teacher, friends, and lovers ourselves, and to give to others, so that when we leave this world, we cml be what we have given.

The wagon wheel reminds us that the pains of growing old are worthwhile. The wheel turns from ground to ground, but not without moving forward. Although we have only one life cycle to live, although it is only a small part of human history which we cover, to do this gracefully and carefully is our greatest vocal.ion. Indeed we go from dust to dust, we move up to go down, grow to die, but the first dust docs not have to be the same as the second, the going down can become the moving on, and death can be made into our final gift.

Aging is the turning of the wheel, the gradual fulfillment of the life cycle in which receiving matures in giving and living makes dying worthwhile. Aging does not need to be hidden or denied, but can be understood, affirmed, and experienced as a process of growth by which the mystery of life is slowly revealed to us.

II is this sense of hope that we want to strengthen. When aging can be experienced as a growing by giving, not only of mind and heart, but of life itself, then it can become a movement towards the hour when we say with the author of the Second

Letter to Timothy:

As for me, my life is already being poured away as a libation, and the time has come for me to be gone. I have fought the good fight to the end, I have run the race to the finish; I have kept the faith. (2 Timothy 4: 6-7)

But still, without the presence of old people we might forget that we are aging. The elderly are our prophets, They remind us that what we see so clearly in them is a process in which we all share. Therefore, words about aging may quite well start with words about the elderly. Their lives are full of warnings but also hopes.

Much has been written about the elderly, about their physical, mental, and spiritual problems, about their need for a good house, good work, and a good friend. Much has been said about the sad situation in which many old folk find themselves, and much has been done to try to change this. There is, however, one real danger with this emphasis on the sufferings of the elderly. We might start thinking that becoming old is the same as becoming a problem, that aging is a sad human fate that nobody can escape and should be avoided all cost, that growing towards the end of the life cycle is a morbid reality that should only be acknowledged when the signs can no longer be denied.

It is not difficult to see that for many people in our world, becoming old is filled with fear and pain. Millions of the elderly are left alone, and the end of their cycle becomes a source or bitterness and despair. There arc many reasons for this situation, and we should try to examine them carefully. But underneath all the explanations we can offer, there is the temptation to make aging into the problem of the elderly mid to deny our basic human solidarity in this most human process.

Maybe we have been trying too hard to silence the voices of those who remind us of our own destiny and have become our sharpest critics by their very presence. Thus our first and most important task is to help the elderly become our teachers again and to restore the broken connections among the generations.

The elderly or our "elders" are truly our teachers. They alert us to the dangers or decisions which can affect the process of living toward fulfillment in later years. We are all in "the process of becoming" as Carl Rogers would say. The value or our process will be in direct degree to how much we learn to live. The elders can show us that growing older is not the pathway into darkness but the highway into light and enlightenment.

We want to talk about the elderly and their pilgrimage into aging so that we can appreciate and see them in a new way and they can help us, in turn, see ourselves, as we mature, with a new intimacy und understanding.

We want to talk about "positive aging" and "successful aging" which makes the maturing process not a reason for despair but a basis for hope, not a slow decaying but a gradual graduation, not a fate to be struggled with but a future to be welcomed and embraced.

We want to talk about aging and the need for caring and compassion. But it is a caring and compassion which begins with ourselves, so we are able to care and have compassion toward others. Nothing can happen through us, until it has happened to us. Real care and compassion takes place when we are no longer separated by fears, bias, and tradition, but when we have found each other on the common ground of the human condition, which is mortal but, therefore, very, very precious.

Assessment

Chapter 13 Discussion

Discuss the essay regarding Aging by Dr. Veon and on the role of elderly people in your own life as sources of wisdom.

End of Life

Attention

Humor and Death

Why do we joke so much about death? Does joking make it easier to deal with? Inevitably, all of us will have to face the death of many people we know and love and then ultimately face our own end.

Humor about death can provide us with three things:

1. Relief for our own anxieties about death.
2. Help with coping with the death of others.
3. Ease the stress that often accompanies and surrounds grief.

Learning Outcomes

Upon completion of this Chapter, students should be able to:

1. Write and reflect on a personal obituary.

Teaching

Healthcare and Dying

Curative Care is the delivery of medical services with the intent on overcoming disease and/or illness. **Palliative Care** is the delivery of medical services to provide comfort and relief from physical and emotional pain to patients throughout their illness. There comes a point in the disease or illness process that people may choose to only receive palliative care without any curative care. Services that have evolved around this approach have come to be known as **Hospice Care**.

Hospice

Hospice involves a team of medical care providers, volunteers, and other important people to provide terminally ill patients with medical, psychological, and spiritual support through the dying process. Hospice services also focus on family and caregivers through this process.

Maine Hospice Council

The **Maine Hospice Council** is the central advocacy, policy development, and educational center for palliative and hospice care in Maine. Initiatives within this organization include:

1. Hospice/Veteran Partnership
2. Maine Physician Orders for Life Sustaining Treatment Coalition (a project to create ways to enforce patient choice in the use of life-sustaining efforts.)
3. The Maine Pain Initiative
4. Hospice and Corrections
5. ALS Maine Collaborative

Advanced Directives

According to Maine Health

"Under Maine law, the term "advance directive" means any spoken or written instructions you give about the health care you want if a time comes when you are too ill to decide. Should you become too ill to make choices about your care, an advance directive will let others know which treatments/interventions you want and which you do not.

"A health care Advance Directive can give you and your family peace of mind. Documenting your health care wishes spares loved ones the burden of making tough end of life decisions.

"Advance directives allow for many choices. By completing an advance directive, you can identify treatments you want/don't want, state your wishes about donating your body, organs and/or tissues at death, outline your wishes about burial and funeral arrangements, and even state your wishes about resuscitation."

Access copies of Advanced Directives from the Maine Hospital Association

Human Development and Dying

While the process dying is certainly a major transition in life for the person who experiences it, it is also a transition for other family members and caregivers. Throughout this course we have been talking about identity, and identity is closely timed to others in our lives. When people get sick and die our identity in relation to those individuals change.

Maine Grief Support Centers

Caregivers

Many people understand the role of parents caring for their children, but when the parent ages, there may be time where the roles reverse, and the children become the caregivers for their parents. The same applies to spouses and partners who may transition from a partnership role into a caregiving role.

Even though many people may embrace these new roles with each other, any transition in role can create strain.

As a social worker in home care, a principal focus of my work was to ensure that caregivers provided the support and care they needed to continue the very important work that they are doing. With support and shared responsibilities, family members can work together to transition through the process of dying very successfully.

However, there are times where the strain of the changed role can become too much to bear. Reluctant to have the patient placed in a facility, caregivers can become quite fragile and sick themselves. Sometimes this process can lead to problems such as abuse and neglect of the patient.

Loss of Children

There is probably no greater sense of loss than that of a parent losing a child. Parents may experience intense grief that may last for years and perhaps the rest of their lives. Trauma will sometimes create a sense of the world being "wrong" and "unsafe", and the death of a child can create this sense of trauma.

Loss of Parents

At one point in our life, we have to face the loss of our own parents. While this is an expected transition among children who are adults, it can happen when children are young as well.

The loss of a parent while still a child is associated with some adjustment problems including:

1. Persistent difficulty in talking about the dead person.
2. Persistent or destructive aggressive behavior.
3. Persistent anxiety, clinging, or fears.
4. Somatic complaints (stomachaches, headaches, etc.)
5. Eating disturbance.
6. Marked social withdrawal.
7. School difficulties or serious academic reversal.
8. Persistent self-blame or guilt

9. Self-destructive behaviors.

Of course, this can all be happening in the context of an entire family dealing with the death of the parent. When talking to children about death, it is important to use real words and be straight forward about what is happening and involve them in the processes.

Rituals, Rites and Religion

Tasks of Mourning

When experiencing a loss there are four tasks that the mourner needs to accomplish:

1. Acceptance that the loss has occurred.
2. Working through the pain and grief.
3. Adjusting to life without the deceased.
4. Starting a new life while still maintaining a connection with the deceased.

Support groups, religious practices, community connection, and family/friends are key to helping with these transitions.

Cultural Aspects of Dying

Dying is, of course, a cultural universal, and all cultures have developed rituals, rites, and processes to deal with it. In Western culture we may be familiar with such rituals as funerals and wakes associated with death. Some of these are deeply tied to religious traditions.

When someone Dies

When a person dies, there are cultural processes by which we inform members of the community. These happen with civic organizations, churches, and most commonly, through the obituary pages and resources in the newspapers and on the web.

Obituaries are brief descriptions of the person's life that provide the reader with a glimpse of the individual, who they were and their surviving family members. People who are in the process of dying often write their own obituary, or it falls to a member of the family.

Central Maine Obituaries

Visit this page to read some obituaries

Funerals

Funerals are organized gatherings of individuals associated with the person who has died. These can occur at a funeral home, in a religious center, or even at the grave site (or just about anywhere.)

The ritual is to have people gather to share their sense of loss and provide communal support to the family and friends of the person who passed away. This is sometimes associated with a **wake** or a **viewing** where people can come and spend time in the presence of the body (or ashes) of the person who has died.

Burials and Cremation

In many cultures the body of the person who has died is prepared in some ritualistic way. Icons such as coffins and urns (for the ashes of someone who has been cremated) are symbols of death in our culture.

MOVIE - Behind the Scenes - Funeral Home

Cemeteries are areas of land where individual bodies are buried or placed in a **crypt**. These rituals are pragmatic as much as they are sacred and part of the cultural process of mourning.

After a person dies, their body begins to decompose. The preparations that go into burials and cremations provide for a way to deal with the decomposing body in a safe, honorable, and healthy way.

Religious Rites and Practices

Information on the practices related to death for a number of religions can be found at https://religionmediacentre.org.uk

This site contains detailed information about the rituals associated with Buddhism, Christianity, Islam, Hinduism, Judaism, and Sikhi.

Assessment

Chapter 14 Assignment - Obituary

Purpose

The purpose of this assignment is NOT morbid! The purpose is to highlight the facility of life and reflect on the importance of relationships and connections in your life every day.

Skills and Knowledge

You will demonstrate the following skills and knowledge by completing this assignment:

1. Reflect on your expectations and planning for your own death.
2. Write an obituary.
3. Reflect on the wisdom gained by this assignment.

Task

The basic task of this assignment is to write your own obituary! As weird as this sounds, I really encourage you to think deeply about the process.

You will be examining this assignment as if you died the day you write it, at your current age, with your current situations going on as they are. Using the rubric be sure to include all the elements that I am looking for you to reflect upon.

Criteria for Success

Use the rubric below as a guide to this assignment.

Title Page — 10 points

Standard title page with name, date, course, college name and the name of the assignment…should also include a picture of you.

Cause of Death — 15 points

Your obituary should include your "cause of death" and how old you were.

Family — 15 points

A detailed description of the family you leave behind.

Accomplishments and Goals — 15 points

A description of the accomplishments you have had to date, the goals you had set but did not get to attain.

Funeral Planning — 15 points

Outline how you want your funeral to be held. Be as detailed as possible as if you were leaving instructions. You should also include the date of the funereal, etc.

Reflection — 15 points

A description of your feelings and thoughts associated with this assignment. What was challenging? What should we do with this perspective as we approach our own lives each day?

Mechanics — 15 points

Spelling, syntax, and organizational structure of the paper. Clear and organized.

The Search for Meaning

15

Attention

Viktor Emil Frankl

1905-1997

Frankl was an Austrian born neurologist, psychiatrist, philosopher, author and Holocaust survivor. In his model, a person's search for meaning is the driving force of human development and behavior.

Learning Outcomes

Upon completion of this Chapter, students should be able to:

1. Discuss the relationship between peak experiences and personal world-view.
2. Reflect on Viktor Frankl's authentic interactions, giving back, and attitudes as a part of a personal search for meaning.

Teaching

Meaning

There really is no better way to end this story of development than with asking the most profound questions we have been asking ever since humans took note of the stars and realized how small they were were in comparison.

Philosophers, song-writers, poets, and, yes, even psychologists have been asking those questions"

Who are we?

Where do we come from?

Why are we here?

Since psychology has its earliest roots in philosophy, the search for meaning has been a core, though often underlying motivation for research to understand how we tick! Religion and superstition has always provided ready answers to these questions, but our critical thinking minds wanted to see the evidence.

If anything, following on the footsteps of all the other sciences, early thinkers felt that if they examined God's greatest creation (human beings) then maybe we could understand God!

Maslow and his Hierarchy

We are going to revisit Maslow's famous "Hierarchy of Needs" but we are going to focus on the work her did with the concepts of self-actualization and peak experiences. This is likely the most well known psychological dogma of psychology and we have all been impacted by it.

At the top of most graphic representations of Maslow's hierarchy you will see the phrase "Self-actualization". We encountered this phrase when we discussed the drive toward love and intimacy and when we explored Carl Roger's model of the congruent self. It's time to dive a little deeper. According to Maslow, the driving force behind human behavior is to become self-actualized. From this point, and from this point only, we can transcend our human limits and reach our full potential.

Maslow felt that self-actualization was actually quite rare. Most people did not achieve all the things they wanted to do, all the things they could do...thus, maximizing their potential. Through this process they begin to develop personality traits that are immediately recognizable.

Self-actualized people:

1. have peak experiences (more later).
2. possess self-acceptance and a democratic worldview.
3. are realistic.
4. tend to be problem-centered.
5. are autonomous.
6. enjoy solitude and privacy.
7. have a philosophical sense of humor.

Self-actualization
desire to become the most that one can be

Esteem
respect, self-esteem, status, recognition, strength, freedom

Love and belonging
friendship, intimacy, family, sense of connection

Safety needs
personal security, employment, resources, health, property

Physiological needs
air, water, food, shelter, sleep, clothing, reproduction

8. are spontaneous.
9. enjoy the journey, not just the destination.

Maslow further clarifies that above self-actualization, the true driving force of our lives is transcendence. He felt that individuals experience transcendence through what he termed, peak experiences.

Peak Experiences

Maslow felt that these unique, highly-charged, emotional experiences, were often transformational and allowed the individuals to observe circumstances from an entirely different perspectives. Other peak experiences happened in occasions of **flow**, the characteristic state of consciousness when someone is totally focused and engulfed in a task.

Consider this list of the feelings that come from peak experiences and reflect on your own experiences. Have you ever had an experience that left you with this sort of consciousness?

- Sense of unity of the self.
- Oneness with the environment
- Experience of peak power.
- Non-forcing.
- Self-determination.
- Free of inhibition.
- Spontaneity
- Purposeless creativity.
- Timelessness
- Pinnacle of individuality
- Merging of I and Other.
- Unmotivated by needs.
- Artistic expression.
- Sense of completion.
- Playfulness.

- Surprise happenings.

Please note - the attractions that some people find with doing recreational drugs is linked to our natural quest to have experiences such as these. Drugs, however, are often less fulfilling, and of course, many have other dramatic and negative consequences.

Man's Search for Meaning

In 1946, Viktor Frankl published the book *Man's Search for Meaning* that chronicled his experiences as a prisoner in Nazi concentration camps. Frankl observed what happened to people as they were admitted in the camps.

He observed that they went through three distinct stages.

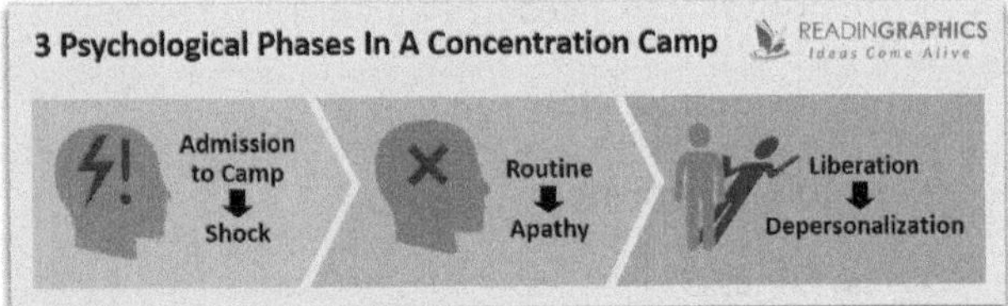

He also observed:

"We who lived in concentration campus can remember the men who walked through the huts comforting others, giving away their last piece of bread. They may have been few in number but they offer sufficient proof that everything can be taken from a man but one thing: the last of human freedoms - to chooses one's won attitude in any give set of circumstances - to chose one's own way."

This impacted Frankl profoundly and he later wrote that these choices embodied a way of coping with even the most horrific of circumstances. These coping mechanisms would replace the "apathy" described in the phases that most people would go through, and would

MOVIE - Maslow on the topic of Peak Experiences

provide the individual with a way to escape depersonalization when they left the camps.

Later, as a contemporary of Maslow, Frankl contended that self-actualization was not the ultimate goal but transcendence. The kind of transcendence he encountered in the concentration camps when he experienced the men he described.

According to Frankl, meaning can be found through the following processes:

1. Experiencing reality by interacting authentically with the environment and with others.
2. Giving something back to the world through creativity and self-expression.
3. Changing our attitude when faced with a situation or circumstance that we cannot change.

Frankl and Maslow

At the last, we are left with both Frankl and Maslow providing us with a model of self-development that leads to transcendence. Meeting our needs, of course, are important, but as observed by Frankl, meeting others' needs is even more powerful. We can even consider each of our needs outlined in Maslow's hierarchy from the point of view put forth by Frankl. Consider, for example, how a person would approach their "esteem" needs by:

- Authentically interacting in their different environments, particularly with the people in this environments.
- Giving something back to the world (our family, our work, our community) as a path to esteem.
- Changing our attitude about the self-focus of esteem and that we achieve, at least in part, because of others.

Assessment

Chapter 15 Discussion

In this discussion we are going to share our peak experiences. We are not going to share the ones that we may have experienced due to substance use of any kind. Consider authentic peak experiences in your life and how these have contributed to your world view.

Chapter 15 Quiz

1. Consider Frankl's three areas necessary for the search for meaning (authentic interactions, giving back, and attitudes). Describe how this aligns with your own experiences in your personal search for meaning.

Special Assignments

Planning to Age Well

Purpose

The purpose of this assignment is to apply the knowledge gained from this class to evaluate current behavior patterns, trajectories, and planning in order to, in a phrase, age well. By "age well" I will start with the knowledge and insights gained through the ongoing, longitudinal Harvard Study of Adult Development.

This study of over 700+ men (and spouses) and young boys from Boston's poorest neighborhoods since 1938 has produced one of the most significant collection of findings on healthy living in late life. These findings are relevant in early life because the choices we make in early life impact the quality of life we will have later.

What makes a good life?
Lessons from the longest study on happiness

The video I have included is a TED presentation from the Director of the Harvard Study of Adult Development, Dr. Robert Waldinger. Dr. Waldinger provides us with a brief introduction to the results of a study over 75 years in the making. What does it take to have a good life?

He starts by saying that recent studies show that people today set goals to attain the good life through wealth and possibly fame. We have been drawn into the lifestyles of the "Rich and Famous" and picture of happiness and satisfaction that accompanies it. We also know the tragedy that sometimes happens when these individuals fall…their descent is as public as their ascent…and it is rarely pretty.

The point is that wealth and fame may be good but they are not the cause of the good life. The Harvard study reveals that relationships with family, friends, and community is what provides us with the good life. Let's look at some results from the the study:

- Individuals who enjoyed good relationships with family, friends, and community were more happy and more healthy.
- Individuals who have maintained these connections are happier.
- More isolated individuals were not only less happy, but they experienced more physical and mental decline earlier in life.
- In our primary relationships, ongoing conflict is the most destructive force. Those who got divorced fared much better than those who stayed in negative, conflictual relationships.
- Looking at people at age 50, the study found that cholesterol, weight, heart conditions, etc did not predict happiness or unhappiness at age 80. Relationships did.
- Finally, in retirement, those who actively replaced workmates with playmates were more happy.

Family, Friends, and Community

This informs us that our connections with others is the most important factor for our happiness...at least according to this study. So, for the first half of this assignment I'm going to have you reflect on your plans to nurture positive connections, with family, friends, and community NOW in preparation for your future.

Finances

Even though the study very much predicts that wealth does not predict happiness, there is ample evidence that poverty does contribute to unhappiness. When I discuss the term "poverty", many of you may feel that you are probably immune to that eventuality. Certainly, living in this country, we don't see the incidence of abject poverty that we might see in war torn areas of the world. It is here, but not to that degree.

The poverty that I'm speaking of is the occasion upon which you arrive at retirement and you realize that your Social Security and savings are simply not enough. Aside from not meeting the basic needs of life, they may be insufficient for you to be anywhere close to calling these the "Golden Years".

Social Security

The Social Security Act was signed into law in 1935. It was a "comprehensive package of protection" against the "hazards and vicissitudes of life". At the time it included unemployment insurance, old-age assistance, aid to dependent children, and grants for states to provide various forms of medical care.

Historical Background and Development
of Social Security

It was never conceived as being a replacement for financial retirement planning. Read that line a couple of times!

Retirement Planning

For many of you, thoughts about retirement might be in the area that Marcia categorized as "Diffusion"...kind of on the back burner. It is this very time where careful planning could help you have a more successful end of your working career.

Keep in mind that the younger you begin this the better, but there is no age that is "too late". Planning for retirement should be a top priority at any age.

To help with this process, I'm going to ask you to spend some time on a very useful and helpful website that I have found.

Skills and Knowledge

You will demonstrate the following skills and knowledge by completing this assignment:

1. Identify strategies to enhance relationships with family, friends, and community.
2. Identity strategies to transition successfully out of work and into a post-work identity.
3. Using online resources, describe a financial plan that will allow you to support yourself after you retire.
4. Explore real-world options for financial planning.

Task

Part 1 - Relationships

For this part of the assignment I'm asking you to reflect on your current state of family, friend, and community relationships. The QUALITY of these relationships are much more important than the quantity. Consider these possible areas of interest:

- Am I in a happy and supportive primary relationship?
- What is the quality of my relationships with my parents, siblings, and other blood relations?
- What is the quality of my friendships with people outside the family?
- Are there people I can count on in my life?
- Is it easy for me to fill in the "In case of emergency call…" question?
- Do I harbor negative feelings toward individuals who are family or ex-friends?
- Am I lonely?
- Do I have connections with my neighbors?
- Who do I know in my community that I can rely on?
- Are there community events or organizations that I would like to be a part of?
- What are the important qualities of my community that will support me as I age?
- Do I have friends outside of work?
- What would I do with my time if I didn't have work?
- What hobbies have I wanted to get into?
- Do I have activities that I currently do with friends outside of work?

This is not meant to be a task of simply answering these questions. These are just ideas for you to reflect upon.

Write an organized, short essay about your status and plans for change in regard to your relationships with family, friends, and community.

I want your essay to be organized with bold headings:

Family

Friends

Community

Activity and Post Work Identity

Under each heading write out your status and planning for a good life.

Part 2 - Financial Planning

To engage in a discussion about retirement planning, I want you to complete an activity predicting the amount of money you are going to need when you retire, and an evaluation of how well you are doing to prepare for that.

The link below will bring you to a retirement calculator that will allow you to analyze your current savings and investments agains your anticipated lifespan, expenses, and retirement needs. Many people, unless they have planned already, find that they fall way short of having a good projected income for late life...but that is why we do it in this class!

So here are the steps to participate in this activity!

Step 1 - Gather Information

You are going to need your **current age** and the age you want to be when you retire (you will be able to play around with these numbers once you enter them to envision different scenarios.)

To determine the number of years you will need to live off retirement income you are going to have to **predict your death!**

To predict your lifespan you will use a handy calculator published by John Hancock Insurance. Simply answer the questions and your expected lifespan will appear on the right.

John Hancock Insurance Lifespan Calculator

I was born in 1965 and my expected lifespan was to 94. If I want to retire at 65, will need to account for 29 years in retirement!

You want your **CURRENT household income** (you can also use your PROJECTED household income anticipating the job you will have in the future.)

Next, you want your **current retirement savings** (how much do you have set aside right now.) This might be a zero number if you have no current retirement plan or savings.

Step 2 - Calculate your Anticipated Income Needs

In this step you want to account for the bills you are going to have when you retire. Some expenses will go down (less driving because you are not working), others will go away (you should not have any student loans anymore!) and some may increase (medical and medication expenses.)

Try to be as honest as you can. Better to create a bad situation and plan for it than a good (and unreasonable) expectation and fall short.

Here are some expenses you want to keep in mind:

- **Required Expenses**
  - Shelter
  - Food
  - Healthcare
  - Clothing
  - Utilities
  - Transportation
- **Optional Expenses**
  - Travel
  - Hobbies
  - Entertainment
  - Dining out

- Donations
- Subscriptions
- Gifts
- Club dues
- Etc.

Create a grand total of these expenses and then determine the percentage of your current income (annual) this is.

So, let's say I have a $50,000 current income and my anticipated expenses are $25,000. I will need to be sure I have 50% of my current income coming in when I retire.

You also want to select a percentage of your CURRENT income that you are willing to set aside for retirement.

Step 3 - Enter the Information

Visit the Retirement Calculator website.

Bankrate Retirement Calculator

Feel free to play around with different numbers in this website. Making a small adjustment such as going from 8% to 10% investment can make a huge different over the years.

I'm not asking for you to report your actual financial plan to me, that is none of my business. However, I would like you to write a brief essay on what you learned through this process and reflect how you may address any changes to your financial planning process.

Criteria for Success

Use the rubric below as a guide to this assignment.

Title Page 10 points

Standard title page with name, date, course, college name and the name of the assignment.

Relationships - Family 15 points

Relationships - Friends 15 points

Relationships - Community 15 points

Activity and Post-Work Identity 15 points

Financial Planning 20 points

Mechanics 10 points

Spelling, syntax, and organizational structure of the paper. Clear and organized.

Retirement plan inputs:

Input	Value	Slider scale
Current age:	23	14 — 39 — 64 — 90
Age of retirement:	67	10 — 36 — 63 — 90
Annual household income:	$50,000	$0 — $100k — $1m — $10m
Annual retirement savings:	8%	0% — 33% — 66% — 100%
Current retirement savings:	$5,000	$0 — $100k — $1m — $10m
Expected income increase:	2%	0% — 6% — 13% — 20%
Income required at retirement:	70%	40% — 80% — 120% — 160%
Years of retirement income:	23	1 — 34 — 67 — 100

In this scenario the person is **23 years old** with a lifespan of **90 years**. They want to retire at **67** and will need **23 years of retirement income**.

Current income is **$50,000** with **$5000** in savings. Anticipating **70% of income to expenses** and willing to set aside **8%** of current income toward retirement.

As you can see in the chart below, they saved **$1,371,815**, but they will run out of money by **age 86**. They will need to change their plan a bit to ensure they have money beyond their lifespan.

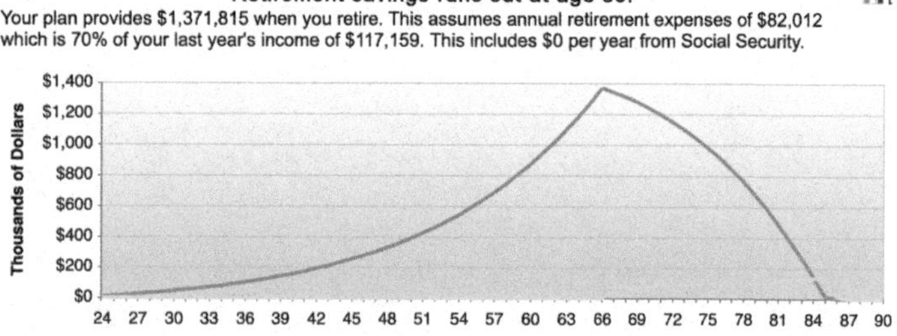

Made in the USA
Monee, IL
03 September 2024

65138122R00151